CONNECT
RELATE
MOTIVATE

CONNECT RELATE MOTIVATE

Master Communicaton in Any Situation

RIK RUSHTON

WILEY

First published as *The Power of Connection* in 2018 by John Wiley & Sons
Australia, Ltd

42 McDougall St, Milton Qld 4064

Office also in Melbourne

This edition first published in 2020 by John Wiley & Sons Australia, Ltd

Typeset in 12.5/14.5pt Arno Pro

© John Wiley & Sons, Australia Ltd 2018

The moral rights of the author have been asserted

ISBN: 978-0-730-38199-0

A catalogue record for this
book is available from the
National Library of Australia

Cover design by Wiley

Printed in USA by Quad/Graphics

VF13253AF-DDE8-432D-B538-15BAE3AF3873_110619

Disclaimer

The material in this publication is of the nature of general comment only, and
does not represent professional advice. It is not intended to provide specific
guidance for particular circumstances and it should not be relied on as the
basis for any decision to take action or not take action on any matter which
it covers. Readers should obtain professional advice where appropriate, before
making any such decision. To the maximum extent permitted by law, the author
and publisher disclaim all responsibility and liability to any person, arising
directly or indirectly from any person taking or not taking action based on the
information in this publication.

To the 'Beautiful One'. Thank you for walking into my life all those years ago, and, more importantly, thank you for walking back into the room after our first 'spirited debate'. As good as it has been since 1983, I know that the very best is yet to come.

Contents

About the author

Rik Rushton is the Best Selling Author of *The Power of Connection: How to become a master communicator in your workplace, your headspace and at your place*, and a TEDx Speaker. He is the Communication Coach and an in-demand keynote speaker on Peak performance, leadership and connection.

He is a 'Recognized Authority' on building growth cultures in elite business and sports organizations. He draws on more than three decades of professional sales, management and business ownership to provide 'time tested' content for individuals and organisations that aspire for their next level.

When Rik is not inspiring audiences across Australasia and across the globe, you will find him with his wife Gai and their three children in the pristine Dandenong Ranges, Melbourne.

Acknowledgements

It's easy to trace the steps to this book coming to life, but it's much harder to acknowledge everybody that played a part in this journey. While the book took only a few months to write, it is based on many decades of connecting with others and gaining the real life experiences that are documented within these pages.

This was a project on my mental 'to do list' for more than twenty years but it was a twenty-minute conversation at a conference I was hosting in Hamilton Island, where it finally crystalised. Thank you to Matt Church for providing the missing piece of the puzzle, *S.A.M. I AM*, I still have the coaster you wrote that diagram on. From that moment, my business manager, Katie, ensured I kept the writing coming and challenged me to get the daily word count to her, as well as providing support and encouragement throughout the whole process.

Once the manuscript was completed, I sent a copy to my friend and celebrated UK author Paul McGee for his review. Two weeks later he contacted me to ask if I had actually written the book personally or if it had been written for me professionally. I took it from that curious line of questioning that it had surprised him in a positive way; a point he clarifies in his foreword. Without Paul's connection to this project, I doubt it would have gone much further, but his introduction to Wiley Australia proved the vital piece to this publishing puzzle.

I have been so fortunate to connect and collaborate with the creative team at Wiley. Thank you to Lucy Raymond for challenging me to take a *good book* and make it a **great read!** Thanks to Jem Bates, Ingrid Bond and Chris Shorten for tightening up the words and putting the real polish on the book, and to Theo Vassili for his astute and valuable marketing ideas. I owe a debt of gratitude and have a deeper appreciation for the power of publishing from working with this outstanding group.

So that's the short-term acknowledgements, but this book has its long-term roots dating back to my primary school years. I actually liked writing short stories and never struggled to find topics to pen! The disruption to our family unit back then and my journey through that painful time gave me more than enough inspiration and motivation to document the lessons learned today. To that end I have to thank my big brother for 'taking me in' after our mother re-married, and practically raising me and continuing to educate me on the important disciplines of life, with none more important than to always say please and thank you.

My brother was my hero growing up and in many ways he still is today, and together with Geoff Everett, I had the two most important male role models in my life at a time when I needed them the most. At this time, I also met my best friend Louis, who is my 'other brother'. He has always been one of my biggest cheerleaders, in partnership with my brother and Geoff. Whether that be professionally or personally, these three men know exactly what to say and do and exactly when to say and do it. I love our weekly chats and laughter.

My 'workplace' changed significantly in 1993 when I was asked to share my success strategies with our company's wider sales team. I prepared for these talks knowing I had only three years of experience while many of the professionals I was presenting to boasted three decades. That day started my professional speaking career and has allowed me to connect with like-minded professionals throughout Australasia and globally. Thank you to all of my professional connections, fellow business owners, trainers, speakers, collaborators and students that have made up my audiences over the journey, giving me the chance to share what I know, learn and do my most rewarding work!

To my mentors including my beautiful godmother Judy Parkinson, Pat Mulligan ('nothing is more important than family'), Chris Bell, George Hateley, Tony Robbins, Dr Denis Waitley, Dr Stephen Covey, David Knox, Bob Wolff, John McGrath and the late, great Jim Rohn, I wrote this book in part to honour you all and to continue to share your wisdom. For Jim Rohn in particular, he made me promise I would write at least one book when the time was right; knowing that would lead to follow up ones, and I hope Mr Rohn's prediction of a book series comes to fruition. According to Jim, 'The magic was that I wrote 5 books ... the mystery was, why didn't I write 25?' He told me that sometimes the book and timing choose the author, and that was certainly the case for me.

Finally, I need to acknowledge the most important person in my life. This book accomplishment is no surprise to my beautiful wife, Gai, who tells me she knew I had a talent for writing from the very first letter I penned to her way back in the early 1980s. She has kept every note, card and letter I wrote to her. We have also written a pretty special story together in the wider journey of life. Her contributions to our story continue to shine at 'our place' with our three amazing kids, Lockey, Chris and Amelia. We could not love you three more and we are proud of the people you are and who you are becoming. I know there are more exciting chapters of love and laughter for us to write together. I will look forward to recording the magic moments that will happen at 'our place' in the years ahead. *The very best is yet to come.*

Foreword

From the moment we take our first breath to the moment we die, we are in some way communicating with the world around us. For all the practice we get, though, not all of us are that good at it. Agreed?

But there are exceptions. You just happen to be reading a book written by one of those exceptions. Rik Rushton. He's an expert on the subject of communication.

Now having been to a few karaoke bars, I realise knowing the words to a song doesn't make you a great singer. Likewise, being an expert on your topic doesn't make you a great communicator. But you can relax. Rik is both an expert and someone who has the ability to communicate his expertise in an eloquent, enlightening and engaging way.

When Rik sent over the manuscript and asked me to write the foreword, I was honoured. I'll be honest with you though, I was also extremely busy. So I decided I would read most of the book and simply scan the rest.

But I didn't. I read it all. Every single word. You see, that's Rik's skill. Through his storytelling and his easy and accessible writing style he draws you into the subject.

As you'll discover, some of Rik's insights are not only profound, but also deeply personal. Trust me, if you don't know Rik when you start reading the book, you'll feel like you do by the time you finish.

Now, I'm fortunate. I know Rik both as a colleague and a friend. We've spoken at conferences together. I know his family. I've stayed at his home. I've even bonded with his dogs, Ted and Ferris! So can I let you in on a secret? He walks his talk. What you see is what you get. On stage or off, you'll meet the same man. And that's important to know. The insights and wisdom you'll gain from reading this book are born of character and experience — they're not just a bunch of untried or unproven ideas and techniques. Believe me, this guy practises what he preaches.

What's really exciting is that the ideas in this book have the potential to change lives. They have the power to change the quality of your relationships both in and outside the workplace. That means with your children, your partner, your family, your neighbours, as well as your colleagues and clients. But first you have to do something with what you learn here.

Rik has played his part in helping you on your journey. Now it's up to you. I dare you to take action on just one of the ideas you discover in the pages that follow. Trust me, it will make a positive difference on your road to success — whatever success looks like to you.

I sincerely hope you gain as much from reading this book as I did. Enjoy!

Paul McGee — The SUMO Guy www.theSUMOguy.com

Introduction

It is not what you do that determines the outcomes in your life. It's *who you are*. Because ultimately, who you are determines what you do. If you're a *giver* in the game of life, your actions confirm this. If you're a *taker*, the same rule applies. If you enter relationships with others to see what you can take from that relationship, your actions reveal this. If you're someone who makes a connection thinking only about what you can give to the relationship, you're one of those rare individuals who gains *everything* from the exchange.

WHO YOU *ARE* SPEAKS LOUDER THAN ANYTHING YOU CAN SAY.

Connection is the keyword here. As human beings, our connections, or relationships, are formed through our ability to communicate. The quality of our life is therefore directly linked to the quality of our relationships. And we need to know how to communicate better if we are to form deeper connections with others, as well as with ourselves.

Communication is one of the most puzzling paradoxes of our time. We live in a hyper-connected world: more plugged in, tuned in and turned on than ever before. Yet social scientists confirm that more and more people feel isolated and disconnected from their communities and even their own families. They feel overworked, underpaid, misunderstood, isolated. Despite being 'in touch' 24/7, many people feel disengaged and disillusioned.

This book offers a roadmap for leaders who want to harness the power of communication to influence their teams and clients, for parents who seek better relationships with their kids, and for everyone who desires deeper and more fulfilling connections with those around them.

Business leaders know all about the struggle to engage and empower a workforce that clocks in then checks out (I call this the *workplace challenge*). How we think as individuals determines how we feel and communicate through our personal self-talk (this is the *head space challenge*). Finally, parents know the challenges of connecting with teenagers who text better than they talk (this is an example of the *your place challenge*). This book delivers proactive solutions to enhanced communication in each of these three critical domains — solutions that are as vital for business leaders as for parents or those seeking closer, more loving relationships.

The Power of Connection presents a fresh approach to tackling modern communication challenges, written for today's time-poor reader, easily consumed in one sitting (one flight) or one night! It takes a holistic approach to professional and personal communication that will be a significant support in your 'workplace', your 'head space' and 'your place'.

Improving our communication skills is a fast track to success in every area of our lives. We can improve our mindset through positive self-talk. The most important relationship you'll ever have is your connection with you! The way you describe yourself in those conversations you have with the little voice inside your head thousands of times a day determines how you relate to and act in the outside world. Deeper connections with those close to you — family, friends, work colleagues, pets, pet rocks if that's the extent of your social group — are formed through your quality communications, first with yourself and then with others. Communication is an *inside out job*.

My aim in writing this book is to provide you with communication tools that will improve every area of your life, as they have mine. This is not just about the words you use, which are only one aspect of your communication. Non-verbal communication is just as important. An exploration of the Power of Connection should begin with an understanding of the first key point:

EVERYTHING COMMUNICATES SOMETHING ABOUT US... THE VERBAL AND THE NON-VERBAL.

It has been my experience that people engage less with your words than with your energy in delivering them. It's your personal vibe that attracts your tribe.

When I meet someone for the first time, I find myself automatically assessing their energy: do they come across as positive, negative or neutral? I can then quickly 'join the dots' from their daily habits. How they think determines how they feel, which determines how they express their thoughts and feelings through the words and actions of their daily communication.

Author Will Durant summed up one of Aristotle's teachings as, 'We are what we repeatedly do. Excellence, then, is not an act, but a habit.' It is perhaps not surprising that an ancient Greek philosopher whose name can be translated as 'the best purpose' should provide us with such a timeless definition of *habit*, passed down through the ages for almost 2500 years. It is the cumulative effect of our daily actions that form these habits. As my mentor Jim Rohn so regularly told me, 'Success is a few small disciplines repeated every day.'

The people I know — those I am lucky enough to associate with and mentor, and those I am even more fortunate to have as personal mentors and friends — share a similar glow. Under the law of attraction, like attracts like. If you are seeking greater success in your life, you need to find ways to improve your verbal and non-verbal communication skills to attract more like-minded people.

Success, in every realm of your life, is not a solo performance; it comes from engaging with other people, and it's no surprise that those with superior communication skills achieve higher levels of success.

ALL SUCCESS IS BASED ON YOUR ABILITY TO CONNECT.

Connection is a pillar that supports every successful person and pursuit I have ever researched in my life! There are no successful hermits.

It is important to acknowledge that when I talk of success, I'm talking about much more than financial prosperity. I have the great good fortune to coach many individuals who by any standard would be considered financially independent. Yet many of them are unhappy; they feel unfulfilled and wonder whether there isn't more to life. They can buy anything they want, except a day off (given they are workaholics), a loving relationship and/or magic with their children.

I know other people who live on Struggle Street, challenged economically on a daily basis, living from week to week, forced to rely on others' support. Yet these same individuals often have strong relationships with their children and are raising polite, passionate and respectful kids, teaching them strong values that will stand them in good stead in the game of life.

Of these two groups, who is the more successful? Is it the person who has unlocked the code to financial success, or is it the person who has unlocked the code to developing a special relationship with their family? Of course it depends on what each person values most. Our wealthy individual may acknowledge that money isn't everything, yet for them it's right up there with oxygen. Our parenting genius may declare, 'No amount of money can replace the relationship I have with my children, and by that measure I have wealth beyond counting.' It's hard to argue against either of these positions.

We all know that there are many pieces to the puzzle of life. All the money in the world cannot buy back your good health, nor can it improve your mindset — on its own. Yet it is important to acknowledge that while money can't buy everything, it can provide you with valuable resources and choices in the pursuit of success.

For me, ultimate success is achieved when *what you do on a daily basis meets your highest values*. I am passionate about holistic success. And I want to convince you that you can have it all, improving all areas of your life — starting with your ability to communicate.

I must admit to writing this book for purely selfish reasons. Not the obvious ones you might think of, such as wanting to be a published author or to position myself as a platform speaker. I've written enough articles as a coach to satisfy the 'author' bug, and have spoken before conference crowds and audiences of thousands since 1995, so I have long since fulfilled that need.

More importantly, I am writing to educate our grand-children (who are yet to be born) in the same way my wife and I would like to think we have taught our three children around the principles of quality communication. In time, we fully expect to become the 'funky grandparents' we always imagined we would be, and I want to document these ideas while I have the time to prepare for this ultimate role.

Our grandchildren will be born into a very different world, and we see our role as grandparents as to ensure they have the skills to communicate effectively in the exciting, fast-paced world they will inherit. We will share with them that raw personal moment you will read about from the very first words of chapter 1. They will learn why, next to love and security, communication is the most vital pillar to successful family and work relationships.

If nothing else, this book will be a lasting reminder for my family, and hopefully for yours, of the power of quality communication. My hope is that from reading the stories they, and you, will learn more about how developing better communication and connection skills leads to a better quality of life.

Quality communication is a lifetime study. Let's now explore together the small improvements that can make the biggest difference in your life through improving your ability to communicate.

CHAPTER 1
Rules of engagement

'Where are you going? I haven't finished yet. Get back here — we need to talk this through!'

I can't remember the catalyst for our first argument, but I can remember clearly the way my fiancée calmly left the room. It was the first 'spirited debate' we had experienced in our five-year relationship. It was a mystery to me why Gai would walk away and leave the matter unresolved. I'm not sure whether I was more angry about our disagreement or her calm exit. Shouldn't the situation stir up a more emotional response on her part?

In the doorway her gentle voice spoke volumes: 'I'll speak with you when you're ready to stop yelling and start talking.'

'I'm ready now!' I yelled back.

'Clearly you're not,' she whispered as she quietly left the room.

THE SOLUTION IS OFTEN FOUND *AWAY* FROM THE EXPERIENCE, NOT KNEE-DEEP *IN* IT!

Not that I knew it then, but the time alone helped me to achieve a major breakthrough that would affect not only my communication with the person I loved more than life itself, but my wider communication from that day forward.

On communication failure

How could two people who had so much in common be so far apart in their thinking? Thinking about everything we were about to embark on in the coming year, including exchanging vows in front of our respective families and close friends, I wondered whether it might be hard to make a lifetime commitment to each other if the first sign of trouble saw one of us retreating from the room. We had only recently got engaged and already I could not imagine my life without her, but I was perplexed by how to resolve what seemed like a serious communication problem.

Even then, in that uneasy moment, I did not question our relationship, just the manner in which we communicated with each other, especially in times of stress and challenge. In the many years ahead of us circumstances would surely conspire to put us in a place of conflict, and we would need a better way of resolving these differences than evidenced in our first poor attempt.

How could we hold such opposing views on the same situation? We shared so much — including, as I will de-scribe, surprisingly comparable upbringings — that the idea of total disagreement on any subject at this stage in our relationship was hard for me to accept. Until that point we had seemed to agree on everything important. In fact, what we had experienced was not so much a disagreement as a communication failure.

Gai and I are both the second youngest of five children. I have a brother and three sisters. She has a sister and three brothers. Both our mothers were adopted. Both were nurses in country towns. Both our fathers were blue-collar workers, men who possessed a higher intellect than their menial jobs required. Both our fathers put their life ambitions on hold to provide secure homes for their families, to feed and clothe and provide for their children as best they could. In both households the weekly pay cheque did not stretch to the end of the week.

We know that both of our fathers went to work under sufferance. At the end of the working day they would each repair to their local drinking establishment (as chance would have it, less than five kilometres apart) and the company of like-minded mates. They didn't go to the pub to 'talk through' their problems; they went to escape them. It was the Australian way. After a few hours of drowning their sorrows they would return home and take out their personal frustrations on the person they saw as the source of their problems — our respective mothers. After all, as they saw it, their wives were the ones who had fallen pregnant and started a family they then had to support, thereby denying them the chance to pursue their own dreams in life. The volatile mix of alcohol and personal frustration more often than not saw ordinary arguments lead to physical violence.

I had assumed, wrongly, that, as long as I did not follow my father's example of resorting to physical violence during an argument, I could justify my fit of temper. Clearly I was mistaken. I thought as a *student* of my environment, as opposed to a *product* of it, I understood the right approach to successful communication with my future wife. Mistake number two!

Growing up with different communication rules

What became obvious once we had reunited an hour later was that despite all the similarities with respect to our parents, siblings and life experiences, we had actually grown up with very different rules when it came to handling disputes. It was imperative that we talk through these differences and produce a plan that we could use in any future conflicts. Part of that plan had to be to build a 'reality bridge' between our two upbringings.

In our household, if I had a dispute with my brother or sisters we had to stay in the room for as long as it took to resolve the matter. No matter how loud we yelled or how physical our body language got (so long as no blows were exchanged), our parents allowed us to resolve the dispute without their passing judgement. (It was a classic case of 'do as I say, not as I do' on my father's part.) Once the argument was sorted and we had left the room, the dispute was never raised again. This was one of our house rules, and I came to assume that this was how all families settled their differences. But I was about to share a home with someone who played by different rules.

In Gai's family, once a dispute with a sibling reached a point of 'raised voices', the rule was that one party leave the room and that they revisit the dispute later when calmer heads prevailed. This was a foreign concept to me.

When she had explained this to me, as she did so clearly and calmly an hour after my outburst, I realised that while we had a common goal of resolving the argument, we had very different ideas of how to get there. I quickly shifted my thinking away from 'judging' her approach to understanding her point of view that nothing positive can be gained from anger. Gai believed that once you remove yourself from a conflict, you give yourself the space and time to think through the situation and arrive at a better solution. It was obvious that our approaches conflicted and were mutually exclusive. When tensions arose between us, I followed a rule that I had observed and followed all my life. Put simply, I chose to stay in the room and plead my case passionately, and insist on a resolution before leaving it. Again, in my thinking, so long as I did not get physically violent I was not doing anything wrong.

Gai, in turn, was following the conflict resolution handbook that she had used all of her life. I didn't know that my yelling broke one of her rules. In fact, in her thinking, shouting at someone was just as abhorrent as physical violence, which I had incorrectly assumed was the real 'line in the sand'. She was also unaware that leaving the room before the matter was resolved broke one of my rules. By walking out she was telling me she did not value my opinion or respect my feelings, whereas in her thinking she left the room because she *did* care about my feelings. Clearly, by following our own personal rules of engagement we were each unknowingly communicating in a manner that suggested we did not care about the other.

If not for this new insight into the differences in our upbringing, I am fairly certain that our relationship would have gone the way of so many marriages in the Western world, where divorce is all too common. We determined to set our own house rules to avoid that outcome. Growing up in a hostile home had caused us both immense pain as children, and we were committed to sparing our own children such a fate at all costs. (I was always a forward thinker.) An hour before, we had been following opposing communication rules. Now, thinking calmly, we were able to set new rules of engagement for our relationship from that day on.

Recognise rules challenges

Later that experience got me thinking. Why did so many marriages end in divorce? My best guess at the time was that, as in our own relationship, most couples were drawn together by attraction alone. Whether a physical attraction, personality attraction, status attraction or simply Cupid's arrow, these relationships are initially based on the attractiveness of the other. And in the early stages of the relationship we tend to pass over any perceived faults our new chosen partners may reveal. We have the expectation that in time, if they truly love us, they will fall more in line with our thinking and make the necessary adjustments.

Once romance gives way to familiarity, however, we tend to notice more how our partner's behaviour breaches rules we hold dear. The challenge is that our partner will be oblivious to these breaches. Indeed, they won't even know these rules exist. I came to believe that most relationship challenges were 'rules challenges'. The problem, as I saw it, was that most couples were using 'the force' to communicate these rules and expecting their partner to possess 'Jedi thinking' to sense the shifts in the force and behave accordingly.

I saw this firsthand with my parents.

'WHAT'S THE MATTER?'

This, from my father, was part question but typically more statement or challenge.

'NOTHING.'

Would be my mother's terse answer.

'IT MUST BE *SOMETHING!*'

He was a sleuth, my dad.

'IF YOU REALLY LOVED ME YOU WOULD KNOW THE ANSWER!'

But he really didn't 'know' and, even if he did, I doubt he had the emotional intelligence to make a real concession and engage in a positive dialogue to find a mutual resolution.

Sadly for my parents and our family, they usually did not know the answers to their relationship questions, nor did they possess the communication skills to help them solve these challenges. Ultimately it was left to the lawyers and a judge to provide the answers during their acrimonious divorce proceedings. Not only did they fail as husband and wife, but more importantly they failed as parents. Their inability to communicate cost them their marriage and permanently destroyed our family unit.

During that painful time, I started to observe other families in our sphere. The happiest families, I noted, were also the best communicators. Both parents were supportive and were each other's greatest fan. They would use positive dialogue with their children to build their self-esteem. They had a pattern of communication and a rhythm to their relationships that had their family interaction in a constant *flow*. More than admiring those families, I envied them.

Growing up in a multicultural society I had friends of different nationalities, many with non–English speaking backgrounds. Some of my best friends were Greek. A few were Italian. One of my closest friends was Pakistani. Then there were the Anglo-Saxons, who of course made up the great majority of the Australian population in the 1960s and 1970s. Visiting their homes and engaging with their families, I started to notice the different communication patterns displayed by each of these 'tribes'.

A clear pattern was emerging among my Anglo friends. Most were in relationships that were formed on the basis of attraction. These couples certainly looked good together, and they seemed to share the same interests. Yet more often than not the relationships ended acrimoniously, often after a few months or years and prior to marriages. Unfortunately a few ended in divorce.

In contrast, my friends from other cultures with strong value systems, religious beliefs and cultural traditions had amazing success rates. They did not need to learn new traditions but rather to maintain old, time-tested ones. The families of the bride and groom came together. In simplistic terms, each family knew the rules of engagement at the time of the nuptials and, more importantly, the parents would support their son or daughter during their transition into marriage.

Armed with these insights, and with the fresh experience Gai and I had shared, for the first time I was able to connect with her clearly and honestly around the rules of our relationship moving forward. This included *things I must always do* as well as *things I must never do* when communicating with her. We agreed that if we wanted better results in our relationship, then we had to ask better questions of each other to remove the guesswork when it came to reinforcing each other's rules. This way we could avoid breaches of these rules and ensure a real balance in the force. We agreed to honour each other's rules moving forward. This kind of communication showed just how much we cared for each other.

One of the interesting insights for me from this experience was discovering that Gai's parents were prone to the same sort of negative dialogue as my own parents. Her father, like mine, would often joke that if his wife did not 'smarten up her act', he would trade her in for 'a sportier model'. It was clear to me that Gai never wanted to hear such talk in our relationship. I also remember an instant when my father, in a sober moment, complained to my mother about how his present job meant he could not pursue his true professional passion. And I clearly remember my mother ending the discussion abruptly by replying, 'These are the cards we're dealt.' Both these examples reveal the power of language. On their own the words might sound neutral. Combined with weak thinking, a backlog of negative experience and lack of a strong belief system, such talk helped send both relationships down the highway to disaster.

Honour each other's rules

Working through that trivial argument between us all those years ago meant that as a young couple we could identify the origins of our thinking, behaviour and communication. The ground rules we set in place then have formed a foundation for our relationship for more than 30 years. Each of us has learned to understand and respect the ideas and motivations of the other.

RELATIONSHIPS ARE EASIER WHEN YOU UNDERSTAND THE RULES OF ENGAGEMENT.

For as long as I can remember, I have only felt comfortable in my professional life when learning something new or progressing to another level. Knowing this, Gai always supports any decision I make in relation to my personal and professional development. Clearly my mother did not have that understanding with respect to my father's professional ambitions. No matter the cost or the time away from home it may involve, my wife always supports my commitment to personal development, as she knows that attending these types of conferences, conventions, workshops and seminars meets one of my 'golden rules'.

Without a doubt our relationship is stronger now than when that initial attraction brought us together in 1983, as friends and family often confirm when they speak of our 'special relationship'. 'What is your secret?' they ask. We simply explain that we have no secrets! That's the reason we have such a fulfilling relationship.

We have set up the ground rules not just for sharing our hopes, dreams and goals but, more importantly, for shaping the way we communicate with each other. We tell our friends that we don't fall into the trap their own feedback implies: we never compare our relationship with others'. Such comparisons, especially if direct, are bound to undermine their relationship.

'I wish we could have as close a relationship as you two' could be interpreted by a partner as 'I wish you were more like him/her'.

Ask better questions

If I had to name one simple thing that will make the biggest difference in your personal and professional relationships, it would be this: communicate your rules of engagement and discover those of others you wish to engage with. In a loving relationship the questions to ask sound like this:

1. 'What must I always do and say to support you in our relationship?'

2. 'What must I never do or say to you in our relationship?'

3. 'What qualities or traits do I need to improve to enhance our relationship?'

IF YOU WANT BETTER RESULTS IN YOUR RELATIONSHIP, ASK BETTER QUESTIONS OF EACH OTHER!

All you need to do is share with your partner the three things that are important to you. 'If I can do these things for you, will you be willing to do these things for me?' Remember that everyone is different, and just because you value something doesn't mean your partner has to. By clearly communicating your values, you are asking your partner to *respect* those values, not to *own* them.

I value time. Other people value money. My view is that you can always get more money, but you can never get more time. Before I communicated this value to my wife, attending functions together could be stressful for me. I always like to be early or at least on time. Gai liked to leave for the function when she was ready and seemed to show no concern for my feelings. It got to the point where I would tell her we needed to leave home

30 minutes before we really did, knowing that we would eventually leave half an hour after the time designated anyway.

When we would eventually arrive at our destination my wife would say, 'What was all the stressing about? We got here on time!' Privately I would be thinking this was due to my driving skills rather than her time management skills. Of course I wouldn't share my thoughts for fear of losing some of the frequent flyer miles I was hoping to cash in later that night. Ultimately, though, I hated playing these games. So I had the tough talk with my wife and communicated how it made me feel when I was placed under 'time pressure', while she pointed out that my stress was making something trivial far more important than it needed to be.

In his great book *Don't Sweat the Small Stuff*, Richard Carlson provides a great perspective on stress when he asks the question, 'Will this be important five years from now?' Five years from now, will it matter that you were five minutes late to an event? Tony Robbins uses a scale metric and asks, 'On a scale from one to 10 where 10 equals death, where does arriving late to a function appear … ?' These are all useful perspectives, but I am kind of fond of Gai's belief that 'stress is making something far more important than it needs to be'.

I'm happy to say that today I display far greater emotional intelligence around time than I did in the past. Gai is also more considerate of my feelings when we are preparing for an event, heading out to a function or getting ready to catch a flight. I did chuckle a few years ago when we were flying home from overseas after a lengthy period away. We were both keen to get home and we got to the airport well ahead of schedule. Arriving at the gate, boarding passes in hand, raring to go, we were among the first to be seated. We stowed our bags, fastened our seatbelts and were ready to fly. It seemed to take an eternity for the bulk of the passengers to board and take their seats. Eventually the cabin service manager gave a cordial welcome over the PA and explained that it would not be too long before we pulled away from the airbridge. A few minutes later the captain came over the PA to add his own welcome. He explained that all of the pre-checks were completed and in order and that it was a very short taxi to the takeoff runway, before adding that once 'the last few remaining passengers' had boarded we would be good to go.

'Why are we waiting for these people?' my wife complained.

'Because their time is more valuable than everyone else's,' I replied, with just a hint of sarcasm.

'It's not fair. They should be ready to fly at departure time.'

Part of me was tempted to remind her of all the times I had waited impatiently for her 'final preparations' before our takeoff to various functions or events, but again I was more focused on my frequent flyer miles when we eventually got home.

Sharing each other's rules doesn't mean there won't be disagreements in your relationship. Conflicts are inevitable in all partnerships. But by identifying and clearly communicating each other's rules of engagement, you take out the guesswork and should be able to avoid major breaches. Even after being together for 35 years we still experience the odd disagreement now and then.

THE KEY IS TO QUESTION THE BEHAVIOUR, NOT THE PERSON. CLARIFY THE POINT OF DISAGREEMENT AND QUESTION *IT*, NOT *THEM*!

Remind each other of the rules of engagement. 'You know 99 per cent of our relationship is great; 1 per cent is a challenge at the moment, but are we going to let the 1 per cent ruin the 99 per cent?' You need to view these few disagreements as further opportunities to enhance your communication and improve your relationship through gaining a deeper understanding of your partner.

I admit this takes hard work, but I have discovered through personal experience that the rewards are more than worth it. Hiring a divorce lawyer and arranging custody of the children would be far more challenging and painful than establishing and sharing some ground rules from the outset that just might head off a major fracture. It's all about choices. First we make our choices, then our choices make us. First we make our relationships, then our relationships make us. And good communication is at the heart of all great relationships.

A rules of engagement checklist

☐ Identify your personal rules and how best to communicate them.

☐ Determine and share rules of engagement with loved ones.

☐ Establish the three main rules on which to base the relationship.

☐ Think about any stress you feel and ask yourself, will it really matter five years from now? Apply the 0–10 scale and the 99/1 per cent perspective.

This chapter at a glance

We all expect the people who care about us to know the rules that determine our behaviour and communication, but as much as they love us they cannot possibly know all our rules. What's more, in the stressful professional and personal environments we inhabit today, these rules are constantly changing, and we cannot always expect our partners to inform us of these changes, just as we don't always inform them. Constantly communicating our needs at least takes the guesswork out of it for our loving partners.

Ultimately, though, you'll need to answer this question: What's more important to you — your rules or your relationship?

Relationships are **easier** when you **understand** the rules of engagement.

_____

CHAPTER 2
Tune in before you broadcast

Developing an understanding of how someone you love evaluates information and their preferred communication style should be something every loving partner seeks to do. Imagine how enriched your life would be if you could gain a deeper understanding with *everyone* you connect with daily. The quality of your life is directly linked to the quality of your relationships. Communication either makes or breaks these relationships. Unless your goal is to become a hermit, improving your communication skills with others must be a priority for you.

Good communication with others starts with quality internal dialogue, or self-talk, which is a product of our thinking. How we think determines how we feel. We can all understand how negative thinking generates negative feelings, which naturally produce negative communication. Everything we see, hear, feel and experience is perceived through and evaluated by our belief system. Similarly, positive thinking naturally generates a positive focus and positive feelings, which translate into positive action and communication.

In simple terms, our version of reality is a creation of our own personal beliefs. As Stephen Covey says in his classic 7 *Habits of*

Highly Effective People, 'We do not experience things as they are but rather as we are.'

That's why two people can share the same or a similar experience and yet perceive or remember it quite differently and draw different conclusions from it. I describe in chapter 1 how a dispute can be provoked when two people unwittingly draw on conflicting rules of engagement. In that case, I saw Gai's leaving the room as proof that she did not value my point of view, whereas for Gai it was a loving act that gave us both some space and so increased our chances of finding a better outcome later.

Our perceptions are our reality

Just as my future wife had a different rule on communicating during an argument, my best friend had a different view on how to deal with the loss of a loved one. We both grieved the loss of our fathers, who died just 24 hours apart. The funerals were held on the same day. Both men were in the twilight of their lives, yet both deaths came as a shock. My friend felt anger, frustration with the doctors who could not keep his father alive, and bitterness over the experience. His pain and sorrow were understandable. My view was that my father had run the gauntlet with his health before the heart attack that finally ended his life. By his own admission, the last decade or two were 'bonus years' for him. I wasn't so much sad that he was gone as glad that he had lived. I thought his life should be celebrated. My friend felt the opposite with his father's passing.

Death is a destination we all share. We don't get to decide when we go, but we do get to call how we live our life, what to believe while we are here and ultimately how to deal with the loss of loved ones. As much as my father contributed to the breakup of our family unit, I still believe he did the best job with the resources he had. Like all fathers, he was a great teacher. We can learn from the negative as much as the positive. Dr Denis Waitley illuminates this eloquently in his outstanding book *The Psychology of Winning* when he explains that all stimulus is neutral until we give it a *value*. What makes an experience positive or negative is our response to it.

What this experience taught me was that the end of someone's life can be a source of anger, pain and loss or of joy and celebration of a life well lived.

WE DON'T EXPERIENCE LIFE; WE EXPERIENCE OUR BELIEFS ABOUT LIFE.

Whatever may be objectively real, our perceptions are our reality. This is not a conscious process. Indeed, many of our beliefs were formed in early childhood and reinforced through our adolescence. These beliefs were influenced by our parents, siblings, teachers, extended family and personal experience. Decisions around what we believe spiritually, the kind of career we want to pursue, our political views, and the sports or other interests we pursue — even to which sports team we will pledge our undying loyalty to — are often made for us by others.

Today, with the benefit of reflection, I can see clearly how most of my beliefs were formed by my sphere of influence. As early as I can remember, I adopted much of my parents' thinking. I loved the same style of music as my mother. I was heavily influenced by my father's politics of the 'left' and voted that way the first time I qualified to participate in the federal election. My father would turn in his grave if he knew I have since voted for the 'right' side of politics from time to time.

Imagine trying to run your current tech platform on an older operating system. We both know it would not function. My political allegiance changed as my thinking changed. Obsolete belief systems still influence how we evaluate new experiences. Certainly some beliefs are timeless. Love, honour, justice and loyalty are examples. Many others could be obsolete at your current stage in life. The old saying went, 'If it ain't broke don't fix it.' Your new mantra might be, 'If it ain't broke it could be obsolete for today.'

BREAKTHROUGHS COME FROM A BREAK WITH OUTDATED PROCESSES.

Personal belief blends emotion and logic

As with many things in life, beliefs need to be regularly upgraded to reflect your new learnings and your current experiences. Personal beliefs have an emotional and a logical component. More often than not a belief starts out much like a theory. You make assumptions based on logical observations and deductive reasoning. In other cases, your belief grows out of an emotional viewpoint that can be supported by logic after the event. I vividly remember an example of this that played out on the national stage.

If you grew up in Australia in the 1980s, you could not have escaped the tragic Azaria Chamberlain story. Just two months old, the baby girl disappeared from her parents' tent at a campsite at the base of Uluru. On raising the alarm, her mother, Lindy, famously cried out, 'A dingo's got my baby!' An exhaustive search that night and through the following days failed to find either the body or any evidence of the whereabouts of the dingo. Lindy would later be convicted of murdering her youngest child; her husband, Michael, was charged as an accessory after the fact. Lindy received a life sentence. Given the media hysteria and the hate campaign against her, she had to be placed in isolation during her incarceration for fear of retribution from fellow prisoners. During the drawn-out legal process it seemed that the whole country had an opinion on the case, and a majority were convinced of her guilt.

I was in my final few years of high school at the time. Our legal studies teacher stated confidently that under the logical test of evidence there was no chance of a guilty verdict. No motive for murder was established, no murder weapon found, no body and no witnesses to the alleged crime. In his considered view, therefore, it was hardly an open and shut case, and indeed was not worthy of going to trial! It became clear that this case was ultimately to be judged on emotion, only loosely justified by logic.

A 1984 Gallup Poll suggested that 77 per cent of Australians believed Lindy was guilty. Many scoffed at her story of seeing a dingo carrying off her baby. They were not only convinced of her guilt but believed she deserved the death penalty. Fortunately for her, the death penalty had been abolished in the Northern Territory and in federal law a decade earlier.

It seemed that, while the lack of evidence pointed logically to the Chamberlains' innocence, a kind of emotional mass hysteria insisted on their guilt. During the trial, Lindy was criticised for showing no emotion. This apparent 'unfeeling' attitude on her part only fuelled popular anger and was interpreted as a clear sign of guilt. Some radical thinkers were convinced that the Chamberlains took their baby to the national park with the intent of sacrificing her in some dark rite of their 'weird religion'. In the 1980s the Seventh-day Adventist faith was not well known, an ignorance that contributed to this type of wild thinking.

So with an implausible story, a strange name (Azaria), an odd religion and an apparently unfeeling mother, the 'emotional masses' were quite convinced of the Chamberlains' guilt. A few years later, Azaria's matinee jacket was found buried next to a dingo's lair. Soon afterwards Lindy was released from jail. Despite her being fully exonerated, a small minority continued to believe that she had committed the crime.

It is this type of thinking that can start arguments within your family and start wars in the wider world! Many of our decisions are based on emotion and justified later by perceived logic. Our personal beliefs are structured around a blending of these two components. Once established, beliefs are accepted as fact and become our operating system, controlling how we process every piece of data we receive. From our earliest days of learning we are taught to form words and sentences but are rarely taught empowering beliefs. And from this platform we communicate both internally and externally.

So all communication is *belief driven*. Control your beliefs and you control your communications. Improve your beliefs and you improve your communication.

MASTER YOUR BELIEFS AND YOU WILL BECOME A MASTER COMMUNICATOR.

The Chamberlain case sparked my early interest in human behaviour and the influence of mass hysteria. I am certain I would have enjoyed studying psychology and human biology at university to gain a deeper understanding of the connection between our thinking and communication skills. But in early 1985, when most of my friends were passionately embracing university or college life, I decided to defer my place after just two short weeks, for two reasons. Firstly, I knew after 10 days of college that I did not want to be a secondary school teacher, that standing in front of a blackboard teaching high-school kids was not for me. My wife still chuckles at that, given how much of my professional life now is spent in front of a whiteboard teaching professionals in various industries.

Secondly, I had fallen in love with a beautiful young lady and wanted her father's permission to marry her, so I decided I needed to make some money fast. With not much more thought than that, I found my way to a local food distribution warehouse and began what I imagined was my quick dash for cash as a storeman and packer. My plan was to make enough money for a first-home deposit and only then to decide on a career. And I foolishly thought that if I lived frugally I could achieve this in under a year. Four years later, my friends were graduating with university degrees and I was learning the harsh lesson that I could not save money as fast as the real estate market was rising. What I did gain unexpectedly, from working in a warehouse that was a melting pot of ethnic diversity, was a great grounding in how to deal and communicate with different personality types!

Flexible communication approaches

Looking back now, I feel like I got a PhD in psychology by default through my dealings with people from all walks of life. Even at the time I thought the communication skills I learned would have prepared me for a role at the United Nations. When you think of factory workers, you tend to think of poorly educated, working-class individuals directed by a management team with conflicting motivations and agendas. That was not the environment I worked in for almost five years. Many of the workforce had a good education, some from the elite private schools in Melbourne, but were questioning 'what life was all about'. They wanted to simplify their lives with an easy job that paid the bills.

I worked with three individuals who had formerly run multinational companies and were burnt out by the corporate world. They enjoyed getting lost in the simple process of packing food items into cardboard boxes and passing them along the conveyor belt, knowing that at the end of the day they could just clock off and go home. I also worked with new Australians who had escaped poverty and persecution in their former homelands and were building a new home for their families.

I quickly understood that you could not communicate with all of these people in the same way and expect meaningful connection. Just as no single radio station could satisfy all listeners and no TV channel could accommodate the interests of every viewer, no single communication approach would work in this environment.

TO TRULY CONNECT WITH THIS DIVERSE GROUP, I NEEDED TO DEVELOP A FLEXIBLE COMMUNICATION APPROACH.

In a workforce totalling in the hundreds, I would spend most of each working day with a crew of three men and a woman. Between us we represented five different ethnic backgrounds. For three of us, English was a second language. Still in my late teens, I was the youngest, while the oldest was in his mid fifties. Each day began when you punched your timecard to show you had arrived before the mandatory 7.30 am start. I was always the second in our crew to do so.

Personality types: colour coding

The first, 'TT', was a highly educated gentleman who was born in London and had found his way to Australia as the Asia-Pacific regional manager of a global company. After two decades working six and a half days a week, TT was burnt out and somewhat bitter about the corporate world. For almost half his life his decisions and directives had shaped the lives of more than 5000 employees and their families. His wife had left him, feeling that he loved his career more than her and their children. Now he relished being able to simply follow someone else's instructions and 'clock on' without having to take his work home with him.

In five years our morning greeting never changed.

'Morning, TT. How are you, sir?'

'Ready to go.'

Always the same three-word *Groundhog Day* response he delivered with force and meaning. And he backed it up with action, packing more units than anyone in our team and, I suspect, anyone else in the entire warehouse. TT valued time more than anything else. Perhaps that's why we connected so easily. He spoke fast and direct. He moved with pace and precision. If TT was a drink he would be coffee, although I doubt that even instant coffee was fast enough for TT. When you were around him you were on red alert. If people could be grouped by colour based on their personality traits, then TT was red.

He was tall and strapping and moved like a man on a mission. When entering a lift, he pressed the floor number repeatedly. It was as if he felt that the more vigorously he hit the button, the faster he would arrive at his destination. TT would finish your sentences for you if he felt you were not speaking fast enough. In the early days of our communication TT would say, 'Can you speak a little faster so I can listen quicker'? During bathroom breaks TT would do his business and start flushing before he had finished. I think he liked me because I too chose a faster tempo in communication and action. And because when I was first introduced to him I shook his hand firmly, looked him in the eye and spoke to him with the respect I thought a man of his background and obvious intellect deserved. Most importantly, I spoke quite fast.

Once I learned of his work background, I was intrigued to know more, and my natural curiosity won him over. One day I said, 'TT, what an amazing professional career you had. Clearly you paid your dues and have earned the right to do whatever you want to do for the balance of your working days.'

'I sure have!' he replied warmly.

'I'm sure I could learn a lot from you. Someone like you with all of your experience, having gone through countless battles, taking your fair share of hits and not just surviving but thriving in the cutthroat corporate world. You could teach me so much.'

I can still see his smile.

There's an old saying that when the student is ready the teacher appears. TT was a passionate teacher, and I was a willing student. Not so much because I wanted to climb the corporate ladder ... I didn't even really know there was one! When I learned of his income level in his former role, I was amazed that he could accept a lowly storeman position. Of course I wanted to generate the type of income he once had! During our daily exchanges TT taught me the value of time — though clearly I failed to pass that on to Gai! He explained in his typical direct way, 'The same 168 hours is available to everyone in any given week. My advice is if you want to raise your income, don't waste any one of them.'

The third member of our crew to arrive for work was PK. If TT was coffee, PK was a decaf version — in fact, make that a double decaf! He was the opposite of TT in every way. Where TT moved like a gazelle, PK moved like a glacier. He spoke slowly and softly. This may have been due in part to the fact that English was his second language, but I am positive it was more to do with his personality colour. Where TT was a raging red, PK was a soft aqua. He rarely instigated a conversation. If he spoke at all he would consider his words carefully, speak in a hushed tone and take a long time to finish a sentence. This drove TT crazy. PK disliked communicating with TT because he knew that TT would always cut him off and finish his sentences for him!

PK avoided confrontation, would never voice an opinion on any subject, and was happiest at the back of the crowd and out of the limelight. Our typical morning ritual would involve a simple greeting and almost always a very 'aqua' response:

'Morning, PK. How are you?'

'Fine.'

There was no point in asking him to expand on that. At best you might extract a 'Very well', which would normally coincide with his tomato plants being ripe for picking, an event that gave him immense joy.

I liked PK for the gentle soul he was. He never had a bad word to say about anyone and looked for the good in everything. While he was short on words, he was very observant of both his environment and the people in it. He knew if you were feeling down, and he would be the first to enquire if everything was okay. I think PK liked me because I never pressured him in any way. Where TT was like a bulldog, PK was more like a refined cat. You had to stay away from PK's personal space until he invited you in. I would find cunning ways to get more invites into 'PK's world'. I would show him an advertisement in a gardening magazine, but rather than place the article under his nose I would wave it from a distance and have him meet me halfway! Once he was in neutral territory he would relax and converse about the beauty of a 'perfect' rose or bloom.

PK loved to garden, to plant from seed and to invest the time required to tend his plants, often over more than one growing season. Where TT valued time, PK valued the process of creating things, no matter what the time investment! They were night and day, as different as red and aqua, espresso coffee and decaf.

The fourth member of our team to arrive to work was Pepe! You knew he was coming well before he entered the room. He was always calling out to workmates, singing or whistling loudly. If one thing defined him, it was his infectious laugh. It was the kind of laugh that came from deep in his diaphragm and exploded like a volcano. Pepe loved life. He loved people and connecting with friends. He was a hugger. He would greet you every morning with a warm embrace and a genuine enthusiastic greeting.

'Hey Pepe! How are you today, my friend?'

'*Heeeey Rikiiiiii!* Never better, my friend.'

That was one of Pepe's more conservative greetings. He had some great one-liners for the purpose. One was: 'Any day above ground is a great day.' Another: 'This could be the last morning we share together, as I feel I'm a certainty in the lotto tonight.' And my personal favourite: 'Well I'm doing better than anyone listed here [he points to the death notices in the daily paper]. Do you notice how everyone seems to die in alphabetical order!' Which was always followed by a belly laugh that could be measured on the Richter scale.

If Pepe was a colour he was golden, like the sun. Very gregarious and outgoing, his personality shone brightly. He was everyone's friend and enjoyed interacting with every team member. Where PK was comfortable at the back of the crowd, Pepe was front and centre, holding court with his animated stories. Where PK spoke softly, Pepe spoke as if addressing a crowd. Pepe was a great storyteller, PK was a great listener. TT had no time to listen.

Pepe spoke at high volume with great animation. You could talk to Pepe for 20 minutes and laugh for 15 of those minutes. He was easily distracted and hard to keep on track. He was always ready for a good time, a laugh or a prank. He communicated best with people who approached him with a smile, which brought a warm embrace and a sparkle to his eyes. I always ensured that my energy levels were high when I engaged with him. Pepe would light up the room the minute he entered it, whereas PK would light up the room ... the minute he *left* it. TT would already have hurried on to the next room!

It was important to use lots of descriptive words when communicating with Pepe and to reinforce these words with hand gestures. He preferred people who spoke with passion and animation, and I always gave him that body language. I'm not sure if it was well understood back then, but I'm confident that if he were tested today, Pepe would be diagnosed as having ADHD! People thought he was on drugs at the time. I'm pretty sure that drug was endorphins, the natural chemical the brain emits in large quantities with gold-type personalities.

The last member of the crew to arrive at work was Lynn. A very methodical lady, every day she would time her run so she could get her preferred carpark close to the warehouse entry point but could clock on just as the start siren sounded. Lynn would bring her prepared lunch and place it in the same section of the staff fridge, away from other people's items. She once shared with me her regular Sunday-night ritual of preparing all the week's lunches in one go, labelling them and placing them in her freezer so she could pull out each one as needed each morning. This was a process-driven lady. She loved the synergy of working in a team and knew her place in it.

You never needed a watch when Lynn was around. Where Pepe had no sense of time, Lynn was a timekeeper, a trait that was appreciated by TT if not by PK. If you asked Lynn for the time she knew it. She would come and get you exactly two minutes before each break, knowing it would take two minutes to walk to the cafeteria. At the end of the break we never had to wait for the bell as Lynn would round us up and have us back at our workstation right on time.

In Lynn's world, 1+1=2, always. She dotted her i's and crossed her t's. I'm sure she would have made an awesome accountant or engineer as she was so methodical in everything she did. In fact, I suspect she was a frustrated schoolteacher, as she would pick up any misuse of grammar and correct any spelling mistakes on any of the paperwork we would fill in from time to time. I half expected to be graded by her at the end of the year. When I thought of Lynn I thought of the blue handbook all new employees were given that detailed the procedures to be followed when working around dangerous machinery. Lynn was very blue in her daily processes. If TT was espresso, PK was double decaf and Pepe was a triple shot (or perhaps a Red Bull), I suspect Lynn was a flat white with two sugars, stirred right to left exactly 12 times.

Speak to their heart

Sorting out my work colleagues by colour helped me with my daily interaction and communication with them. I always seemed to get the best out of each of our exchanges and I'm certain this was due to the fact that I changed my personality to match theirs. With TT I would speak fast, directly and always with great eye contact. With PK I would slow down my patter, adopt a consultative approach and avoid breaching his personal space. With Pepe so long as I had a smile on my face (and a song in my heart) and approached him with energy, I could get him to do almost anything. If I approached Lynn with a question about the best process to achieve the best outcome she would be very generous with her advice, because she felt valued and needed. And when I entered the corporate world for the first time in 1990, I looked for an assistant that had very blue traits, like Lynn.

What I learned from engaging with these different person-alities for five years is this:

WHEN YOU SPEAK TO A PERSON IN YOUR PREFERRED WAY, YOU SPEAK TO THEIR HEAD. WHEN YOU SPEAK TO THEM IN A WAY THAT MATCHES THEIR PERSONALITY, *YOU SPEAK TO THEIR HEART!*

And while I probably didn't appreciate it at the time, in interacting with this wonderful crew I was developing my leadership skills.

Not surprisingly, TT and PK did not engage with each other a lot. Neither did Lynn and Pepe. That's not to say they did not work well together; it's just that they could not work to their optimum level together. TT and Lynn talked a lot, because he admired her process-driven personality and she respected his time management focus. In the corporate world Lynn would have been a great personal assistant to TT. For the work we were conducting, Lynn would create a great plan, TT would lead the way and do the 'heavy lifting' (literally). PK would calmly mop up any mess left behind and could be counted on to stay cool in a crisis. Pepe made the whole experience as enjoyable as you could possibly make factory work! And I interacted happily with each of them throughout every step of the process by broadcasting on their preferred communication channel.

One other notable benefit of working with such a diverse group of people in an intimate setting was that I could learn their language patterns. Adding this to my understanding of their personality colours helped me gain an understanding of how each of them 'ticked'. This was around the time that Bandler and Grinder's work on neurolinguistic programming (NLP) was taking off. It would be a further decade before I would learn this methodology in far greater detail, but by dumb luck I was already following a lot of NLP principles in my communication with my colleagues. NLP identifies individuals' language and personality programming much in the same way as I have been describing in this chapter. Part of the NLP process is to listen for a pattern of language used by the people you wish to connect with and to 'mirror' that language.

TT used a lot of direct visual words. 'Look ...' he would start each sentence. *Look, show* and *see* were his staple words. PK used lots of kinesthetic or feeling words. 'I know people think I'm hard to talk to ... I sense TT is upset with me ... I have a gut feeling that Lynn is going to ask me for a favour.' Lynn would use lots of auditory words. 'I hear what you're saying ... the plan sounds good. Let's talk it through.' Pepe would use a combination of all three. 'Listen, let me show you something, as I feel you'll tell me the right thing to do!'

So I would use picture words when speaking with TT, auditory words when communicating with Lynn and feeling words when connecting with PK, while connecting with Pepe called for a combination of all three patterns of language (although so long as you laughed a lot you probably connected with him no matter what words you used!).

Armed with this approach I would ensure that my conversations with TT were short, sharp and direct. If I could show him a shortcut that saved him *time,* and showed him the greatest respect, he would repay the favour. That's how I developed such an easy rapport with TT. With PK I would ensure I slowed down the pace, tone and volume of my interactions and communicated in a nonthreatening way that gave him a sense of security. By using a lot of feeling words, I could connect with PK when others couldn't. Lynn always appreciated the process by which we exchanged information. She loved my descriptive words and the fact that I really *listened* to her in our verbal exchanges. But Pepe was the one I connected with most easily as we had similar communication styles. So long as I was energetic and amusing and used hugs at greetings and farewells, he sensed we had an empathetic relationship.

Finding the right channel

Much of what I have shared in this chapter flies in the face of traditional advice when it comes to successful interactions with others. 'Just be yourself', we are advised. The problem with that advice is that for every 10 people you meet, only one or two are likely to have similar personality traits and beliefs as you.

IF YOUR GOAL IS TO FORM DEEPER CONNECTIONS WITH FAMILY, FRIENDS, LOVED ONES AND PROFESSIONAL COLLEAGUES, THEN YOU MUST LEARN HOW TO 'TUNE IN' TO THESE PEOPLE BEFORE YOU 'BROADCAST' ON THEIR PREFERRED COMMUNICATION CHANNEL.

If you truly want to connect, you will have to adapt to their needs and be flexible in your approach.

The first step to better relationships with others is to understand the relationship between your thinking and the formation of your beliefs. All communication is belief driven, and one of the best beliefs you can have is that it makes sense to tune in to the other person's 'colour', personality traits and NLP process before you 'broadcast' to them. If you match their colour, mirror their body language and use their preferred dialogue pattern you will find you are in sync. You will share a rapport and will be communicating in a way that strengthens your relationship and enhances trust.

As you read this chapter, you may be thinking about the characteristics of members of your own peer group or identifying your own traits. You may have wondered what colour I was at the time. Based on what little I have revealed of my own personality so far, you could argue equally that I was red or gold in those days. I never really saw myself as a laid-back aqua, and being blue was very much the exception rather than the rule in my personality. In all honesty I think I was then, as I would like to think I am today, orange — a gregarious, outgoing, fun-loving person in a hurry to produce results in line with my potential. (For the aqua and blue among you who are complaining that this is not one of the four listed colours, orange is my personal combination of red and gold!)

As I am a public speaker and someone who can 'talk a glass eye to sleep', you could be forgiven for thinking that I would be very auditory in my communication, but I have always been a visual person, both in the descriptive words I use and in how I retain information. I much prefer seven bullet points that I can review quickly than seven pages of dense detail that I'll probably never read. I connect with and form deeper relationships with people who have energy (red) and humour (gold) and who understand the value of time (red).

There are many other personality profiling systems — DISC® and Myers–Briggs are two of the more prominent ones — but I find them too detailed and complex to use in a hurry (note my red thinking). I prefer the simplicity of the colours! And in my colours program, orange is my default channel. Knowing this in myself means I try to find it in others. What's your colour? Think about your personality traits. What are the personality traits and communication triggers of your family members? By applying the simple formula of red, gold, aqua and blue and the match, mirror and pace process, you will improve your chances of becoming a greater communicator.

PEOPLE ARE NOT THEIR BEHAVIOURS!

One last thought on this topic. Remember that this is not an exact science, and people often don't fit neatly into one of the four personality colours. Someone may display behaviour that seems to contradict their colour. An aqua person may turn red very quickly if they receive a call from their child's school informing them that their youngster is being rushed to hospital after an accident. They will probably run every red light to get to the hospital fast. Weeks after the event, with their child safe and sound, they will no doubt return to their normal aqua ways! People are not just behaviour types — they react to real circumstances as best they can! But all things being equal, people will lean towards their normal ingrained patterns, and tuning in to them will provide you with the best frequency to broadcast on!

A tuning in before broadcast checklist

☐ Life is not a solo performance; we need to communicate well with others to change our life for the better.

☐ All experiences are neutral until we communicate a response to them!

☐ All communication is belief driven. Try to identify the main beliefs that influence your behaviour, as well as the behaviour of loved ones, friends and professional colleagues.

☐ Identify your personality colour and the colour of the people you connect with every day.

☐ The four main personality colours are red (direct people who value time; fast talkers; outcome focused), gold (descriptive talkers; animated communication style), aqua (reserved; quietly spoken and non-confrontational; dislike pressure), blue (process driven; love systems and checklists; prefer logical communication). **For a comprehensive free PDF download on colours profiling, visit rikrushton.com.**

This chapter at a glance

Think of the few key people you spend most of your day with. Can you identify their personality colour and preferred communication style (their words, visual or picture expressions, feelings and emotive vocabulary)? Once you have determined their personality profile, you can broadcast on their preferred frequency for a far greater and deeper connection.

If you truly want to **connect**, you will have to **adapt** to their needs and be **flexible** in your approach.

_____

CHAPTER 3
Adjust your personal programming

One of the most important communication skills you can develop is the ability to help others see more in themselves than they thought was possible. This should certainly be a goal for any leader. Leaders, whether of family, business, church, school or community, have a common goal of guiding people towards better outcomes. One of the main ways they do this is by helping them to see and achieve the very best version of themselves.

I grew up quite poor, both financially and in terms of a good male role model at home, but I was very fortunate to connect with some outstanding teachers, especially in high school. I also made sports teams that had great coaches. The only things I enjoyed during my primary school years were morning recess, the lunch break and afternoon recess. This was when I could engage in my main passion, which was playing sport with my classmates — footy and soccer in the winter, cricket and 'down ball' in the summer. From this daily ritual I developed good hand–eye coordination and general ball skills, which sadly was never rated on my report cards but was always at the top of mine.

Being small in stature meant I had more pace than many of my heavier opponents. I could run pretty fast and, given my lack of size, soccer, where pace was an advantage and a lack of physical weight was no hindrance, seemed to be a better option than Australian Rules. Junior soccer games were among my happiest childhood memories, not just because I could play at a pretty good level in a very strong team, but because we were coached by the first great communicator I really connected with in my life.

GREAT COMMUNICATORS ARE GREAT SIMPLIFIERS!

Mr Fern had a great understanding of the game and an even greater way of communicating that understanding. He possessed all the attributes of an elite coach, and his ability to teach the skills and communicate the game plan was exceptional. His standout quality was the ability to make every player feel like they were *the most important part* of the team.

The three-step process to better communication

I believe great communicators are great simplifiers. I still remember those pre-match sessions in the change rooms. Mr Fern would have drawn the soccer pitch on the board and added each player in their respective position. He would begin by identifying each player's role and his expectations of them for the game in hand. He spoke in a way that suggested he had total confidence in each member of the team to play his part, so long as we followed the process.

PROCESS PRECEDES RESULTS. FOLLOW THE PROCESS AND THE RESULT WILL TAKE CARE OF ITSELF.

Win, lose or draw we would always gather at the end of the game to review our 'process' and the final result. Where Mr Fern stood apart from the other coaches I had in my junior years was in his post-match reviews. Rather than tell us how *he* thought we had played, he would 'tune in' to our reality, asking each of us, 'How do you think you played today?' He would then put your answer in a clearer context and help you draw something positive from the experience.

When a player felt he hadn't performed as well as he could have, Mr Fern would ask him how he had arrived at that thinking. Once the coach had a clear understanding of the player's personal review, he would move the conversation forward in three strategic ways. He would *acknowledge* the player's thinking. He would provide an *alternative view*. Then he would *inspire* the player to improve and find a better version of himself.

» 'Based on your thinking, I can see how you've arrived at that belief.'

» 'Can I tell you what I saw from my position on the sidelines?'

» 'The great news is we have a week to work on improving that area of your game and you are good enough to make that improvement by next week!'

Here's an example: A defender felt he had not played well during a loss. He may have arrived at this 'narrow thinking' because his opponent scored a goal or two. The coach would provide a positive alternative to the player's negative view with an assessment of the wider game.

'Based on how often they got the ball to your opponent in great goal-scoring positions, we're lucky we had you matched up against him, because he would have beaten a lesser player twice as often. The only thing I think you could have done slightly better was force him to take some of those shots from further out. We can work on your higher press positioning at training this coming week, and the good news is we get to see your improvement in seven days' time!'

What our coach was communicating was a different view of the experience, without discounting the player's own belief. He gave a positive focus for the week ahead, inspiring the player to make improvements, with the *positive expectation* he would do better in the next game.

COMMUNICATE IT LIKE IT IS. COMMUNICATE HOW IT CAN BE. INSPIRE THEM TO MAKE A POSITIVE CHANGE.

Conversely, when a player felt he had performed perhaps better then he actually had, the coach would steer him towards the reality of his performance in an empowering way.

For instance, a defender felt he played well because his opponent *did not* score a goal. The coach would once again communicate the message he wanted the player to hear, see and feel.

'By that measure I can *see* how you believe you played well. What I ask you to think about is the fact that you are part of a team. When we concede a goal, we *all* concede the goal. From *my* view, they did not use your opponent much at all when going forward, which could have allowed you to help your fellow defenders to double team their opponents. This is part of *reading the play*. If we focus on that improvement in your game this coming week at training, I am confident that next week your *focus* will shift from beating your opponent to being part of a great defensive team. Today's game proves you can beat your opponent one-on-one. The better news is, once we can add reading the game to your play, you'll become an even more valuable player.'

By following this three-step process and using emotive words, our coach was able to help every player in every position, no matter their skill level, to improve their game and maintain their positive self-esteem. That would be impressive coaching at a professional level. It was truly amazing at junior school level.

Communication by inspiration

I encountered the same process later in my high-school years with our senior football coach. He began every pre-match address by identifying each player, communicating his expectation of their role in the game and providing assurance that they had the ability to execute the game plan. His post-match reviews followed a similar pattern to Mr Fern's. He would tell it to us as it was, explain how it could be, and inspire each of us to make improvements so that every week in each season and over the course of a few years our full potential was achieved.

Both of these coaches had played their respective sports at the highest level and brought a high level of professionalism to local and school sport. And I was the beneficiary of witnessing this better communication firsthand. The same could not be said for my junior cricket coach. Before each game, he would single out only the players he felt were most talented, and if you weren't in that select group you knew that not much was expected of you. No surprise, then, that you would perform accordingly. During post-match reviews, he would tell you how he thought you played, with no consideration of how you may have experienced the game. Even more disturbingly, he had no real concern about how his direct feedback could destroy a young boy's confidence and self-esteem. He would broadcast *before* tuning in!

Of course not all school experiences relate to sport. I was an average student at best in the first few years. By the end of high school, however, I was achieving above-average academic results because I was lucky enough to connect with above-average educators. Schools are full of teachers, but you may be lucky to find great educators. I hit the jackpot by finding two who changed my life.

As already mentioned, I found a great high-school football coach who also was our physical education teacher. There was nothing I would not do or try to please Mr Mac. Indeed, for many years I wanted to be a PE teacher because of him. There are many 'sliding door' moments in life. High school provides plenty of them. During my middle school years 'Macca', as I came to call him, could see that my academic performance did not truly reflect my abilities as a student. He chose to communicate this to me at the end of a PE class early in the new school year. We had just finished a competitive ball game in which I captained the winning side. Macca waited until we were the last two people in the change rooms before he initiated a conversation that would have a massive impact on me for the rest of my time at high school.

'Well done on leading your team,' he began. 'Do you know why I chose you as captain?'

I hoped it was because he felt I had good game and leader-ship skills and he knew I would try hard to win. His response was totally unexpected.

I wanted you to see what the result can be when you focus on leadership instead of just playing the game. I think if you applied the same focus, energy and competitiveness to your academic subjects, you would become a total winner. The scoreboard says you win more often than you lose the games you compete in. Yet in your other subjects, I doubt you even notice there's a scoreboard. But I'm here to tell you there is, and at the moment it's saying you're well behind in the game. The good news is the game is not over. You've got two full years left here. You could be winning on every scoreboard. Then you could be a leader not just at school but in other areas of your life. I'm only sharing this with you

because I see more in you, and expect more from you, and I
would hate to see you fall short of your full potential.

If he had told me this a few years earlier, I doubt we would have
had the right rapport, and his advice would have been wasted
on me. But how could you not be inspired when a teacher you
admired, respected and even idolised took the time to challenge
you to become all you can be? The reason I remember the
conversation so vividly more than 30 years later is that it was
the first time anyone shared the view that they could see more
in me than I could see myself. Not only did I take those words
on board, but I would like to think that I repaid Macca by really
focusing hard on my academic studies. The end result was a
significant improvement in my academic grades.

WHEN THE STUDENT IS READY THE TEACHER APPEARS.

Around this time my year 7 and 8 mathematics teacher,
Mr Everett, was promoted to deputy school principal. I had
always enjoyed my time in class with 'Mr Ev', as we often talked
about sport even if we were meant to be discussing the benefits
of algebra and Pythagoras. Our relationship progressed from
teacher and student in our first year together to mentor and
friend, which I am blessed to say continues to this day. Like
Macca, Mr Ev was an outstanding educator. They both knew
how to *command attention*; unlike some other teachers, both
could get their students to turn up for class, tune in to the lesson
and take positive action by the end of the class.

In my senior years I had developed a new focus on my
academic performance, thanks to Macca. This was not lost on
Mr Ev, who had also enjoyed a period of growth in his
professional career by then. Our regular daily chats about sport
were now conducted in the palatial deputy principal's office,
rather than the modest confines of the classroom. There was a

standing order that no students were allowed inside the school building until just before the commencement of the first period. But the rule didn't seem to apply to me, as every morning began with coffee and conversation in the DP's office.

Mr Ev and I covered all the big issues during these morning meetings — that is, all things relating to sports results, player performances, selection highlights, the highs and lows of our respective football teams, Victorian Football League coaching appointments ... Come to think of it, perhaps we were a bit narrow in our conversational focus!

If my conversation with Macca earlier that year was a sliding door moment, the one I was about to have with Mr Ev was a life-changing one. One day he excused me from the legal studies class and asked me to walk with him to his office. Once there he sat me down and explained that the state Education minister had decided that students should have a say in how their school is run. Consequently, student representatives were to be elected to their respective school councils and to actively participate in the administration of school affairs. 'I think this would be an ideal role for you,' he said.

My idea of an 'ideal role' would be to play sport seven days a week. This just sounded like extra homework to me. Being a student representative at any level was not as high on my agenda as mentally preparing for the fast-approaching lunch break, when I was to resume my not-out innings facing 'Swampy' Collins in a hotly contested session of schoolyard cricket! Swampy was an aggressive fast bowler who had spent the previous hour in our legal studies class taping the tennis ball that would be used when hostilities resumed. The green tennis ball was now unrecognisable under tight layers of insulation tape that made it rock-hard and a perfect fit for his deadly deliveries.

'What are your thoughts?' Mr Ev asked.

My thoughts were I would have to lower my backswing, really dig in defensively and use the pace of the ball to score until Swampy tired and I could play my natural strokes. But clearly this was not the right line to pursue right then.

'Why me, Mr Ev?'

'Because I have watched your development very closely, and I think you are right for this role.'

'How come?' I asked. With one eye on the clock counting down to the lunch break I fervently hoped his response would be brief.

'I watch you interact with others. You seem to be able to connect with everyone, not just those in your year. The challenge will be connecting with the entire school population. That's a key requirement for anyone who fills this role. I believe you have that ability. You don't have to answer now, just think about the opportunity.'

I had the deepest respect for Mr Ev. From the very first assembly he ran as deputy principal, I saw how he could capture the attention of the whole school with just a few words. I had of course watched him do this in the classroom during my first three years of high school, but his use of the power of words to command everyone's attention was a skill I knew I wanted to acquire. I didn't need too much more convincing.

'If I put myself up for this role, would you help me with my speaking skills? I assume I will have to give speeches? I'm not sure if I can do it, but I'll give it a go.'

Mr Ev's encouraging response was exactly what I needed to hear.

'I'm not asking you to consider this position because I *think* you can do it well. *I know you can.* If you approach it in the same way you play your sport, you have every chance of success.'

On being a team player

'Have you ever wondered why you like playing team sport so much?' Mr Ev asked. 'It's because you like interacting with others. Ultimately, this role is about how you interact with others.'

I knew he was right. I loved playing sport *with others*. I hadn't grasped why individual sports such as tennis never appealed to me until Mr Ev pointed this out! It was just one of many key insights he offered during that life-changing meeting. I left his office with the promise that I would give it more thought. Truth be told, I was keen to get outside and assess the playing conditions.

It turned out I had more time to review our meeting than I had expected when, to my horror, I was controversially ruled out the very first ball! To understand the depth of my disappointment and the dispute surrounding my dismissal I need to give you an idea of the playing arena.

The cricket pitch was located in a quadrangle. The wickets were painted on the wall of the woodwork building while a garbage can served as the bowler's end wicket. The subfloor area of the woodwork building had a defined line where the ventilation covers ran. It was a rule that any edge above this line and the batsman was deemed to be 'caught behind' or in 'the slips'. Any edge below this line was deemed not to have carried to these virtual fielders, and you were 'not out'. This had been the rule since Year 7 but now, at the start of our fourth high-school year (Year 10), we faced a conundrum.

While I acknowledged I did indeed edge the ball, it was very clear to my batting partner, 'Dukey', that the ball hit squarely on the line, a fact that was not disputed by the bowler. Swampy's view was on the line was still out. Dukey's view was that on the line was not out. Unsurprisingly, I shared Dukey's view passionately. It occurred to every player involved in this competitive match that after four glorious years this was the first time such a controversial dismissal decision had had to be made. It should also be noted that there were many ways you could be dismissed. Naturally you could be bowled, caught, run out and, more infamously, given six and out if you managed to drive the ball straight back over the bowler's head and clear the fence on the full (which would mean the match ball was now the possession of the neighbouring football club). I carefully avoided that mode of dismissal, choosing as my main scoring zones the shelter sheds on my off side, which favoured my cut shot, and pulling and hooking shots at the neighbouring building on my leg side.

There was no precedent for this potential dismissal and I wasn't looking forward to creating history. Of course this event predated the DRS, Hot Spot and ball-tracker technologies used to validate on-field decisions today.

Normally I would have vigorously defended my corner. It was not uncommon for me to begin batting on Monday morning and still be in Friday lunchtime. But on this occasion I noted the passion in the eyes of two classmates who held strongly opposed views on the issue and saw that what had started as a minor dispute threatened to develop into a major incident.

Whether influenced by my conversation with Mr Ev only minutes before, or overcome by a moment of weakness, I 'walked' (a cricketing term for a batsman who gives himself out). I chose to take that conciliatory action to restore calm and order so the game could go on. Not exactly a 'Mr Gorbachev, tear down this wall' moment, but it was the closest to diplomacy I had come in my high-school years until that point. Maybe I had the makings of a politician after all. And I walked on, straight back into Mr Ev's office, where I was duly appointed 'student representative', a role to which I brought all the focus, commitment and attention I gave to every sporting encounter.

Over the course of the next two years I attended meetings with Department of Education representatives, school principals and student representatives from other schools in our district, presenting the findings and outcomes of these meetings to the school during weekly assemblies. Mr Ev kept his promise and taught me presentation skills, including how to speak in public, using light and shade in my descriptive words, how to speak into a microphone and, ultimately, how to become the best 'team player' I could be.

I think we all experience a day that changes the course of our lives. For me it was the day Mr Ev plucked me from class and explained why I was his first choice as student rep. The next day he told me how he had observed my growth in my academic studies and had continued to follow my sporting achievements with great satisfaction. He was convinced I could achieve the next level of my leadership skills by being exposed to meetings with adults, helping to form policy and communicating that policy in a public forum.

The experience proved invaluable. The positive input from most of the teachers I engaged with went well beyond the classroom to a level that would gratify any parent. Like Macca, Mr Ev saw much more in me and for me than I could ever have imagined for myself. Essentially, he started my career as a public speaker. Without their support, I would not enjoy the quality of life (both professionally and personally) I do today. From that day on, my ambition moved beyond being a PE teacher to a commitment to becoming the best 'servant leader' and 'communicator' I could be. And I owe much of that to Mr Ev.

THE TWO MOST IMPORTANT DAYS IN YOUR LIFE ARE THE DAY YOU'RE BORN AND THE DAY YOU KNOW WHY!

Today I am living proof that 100 per cent of your success comes from your ability to communicate. If not for the intervention of these two elite educators, I can't imagine where my life would be today. I have a very clear understanding of why I do what I do. The skill set that qualifies me to address audiences both nationally and internationally as an educator, motivational speaker and conference host can be traced back to those sliding door moments with Macca and Mr Ev. How fortunate was I?

I have continued to express my gratitude to them both. Indeed, Mr Ev is an important part of our family today. He's like a surrogate grandfather to our three children, taking a particular interest in their sporting pursuits. Next to my older brother, Mr Ev is the most influential male role model in my life. If I continue to acknowledge this debt for the rest of our days together, it will still not go close to repaying his gift to me at that defining moment.

In 2004, when I was Peak Performance Coach of the Western Bulldogs football club, I enjoyed a long-overdue lunch with Macca who, having retired from teaching to pursue his passion for coaching in the elite AFL system, was the head coach of the AFL–AIS Academy program. I think the fact that I had a role with the same professional football side that he had once played for made Macca proud! He deserves a fair chunk of the credit for opening the door to a role in a professional sports club for me. He was pleased I had taken the time to reconnect with him. Teachers hope they make an impact on their students, he told me, but unless the student makes the time to say so, they really never know.

THE BEST WAY TO THANK A MENTOR IS TO SHARE THEIR LESSONS WITH OTHERS.

Many years later I was lucky enough to coach my two very sporty sons in their formative years and early domestic teams in various sports. I knew the impact a good coach and communicator could have not just on their 'game time' performance but more importantly in the wider game of life.

Find out what's important to them

Both our sons loved cricket and showed above-average talent (although I doubt either of them could have endured a week-long barrage from Swampy Collins and his infamous taped tennis ball). Having a good understanding of the game as I did, and knowing through personal experience the benefit of the three-step coaching process, I was confident I could make a positive difference — firstly as their sports coach, but more importantly as their father.

The same was true for football, then soccer. Even basketball. This was a sport I did not play at any level, yet both our sons' first team experiences were in this sport. Whatever sport the boys played I got to coach them outright or at least take on an 'assistant coach' role. I had no intention of coaching their basketball teams but ended up taking on both these roles.

On the first occasion, I approached our older son's basketball coach to offer him what I thought would be welcome feedback on the way he spoke to seven-year-old boys. No doubt he understood the game, but equally clearly he had no understanding of how to communicate it. He would yell instructions from the sidelines and call out their mistakes. He would even shout at the top of his voice, 'Don't miss!' when one of his players was taking a free throw! Not surprisingly, his players were afraid of making mistakes and therefore lacked the confidence needed to play the game well.

I thought he might usefully consider the three-step approach I benefited from as a young lad. To my amazement his terse response was, 'If you think you can do a better job, be my guest!'

And with that brief exchange a new coaching appointment was made.

Now I was coaching a team of boys I didn't know in a sport I had never played, and with absolutely no knowledge of the rules. What I did know something about was the rules of communication. And that was my starting point.

With every kids' sports team I have ever coached, I begin by asking each player what they would like to achieve in the season ahead. For some players, it's the lofty goal of winning the championship or topping the table. For others, it's winning a trophy. For the majority, though, it's simply kicking a goal, shooting a basket, hitting a six or taking a wicket.

So knowing what was most important to each young basketballer became the foundation of my coaching approach. I will admit that those early days were challenging for me. I made some basic mistakes: for example, I didn't realise your team had to be in possession of the ball before you could substitute a player. ('Sub, please.' ... 'You don't have the ball!' ... 'Next sub when we do, please.') But week by week we all got better, especially once the coach had learned the rules.

During the game I would ask the players, 'How do you think we're going?' They would give me their feedback. I would add mine. We would play out the game and then review the performance. In every sport I would follow the same process I was shown all those years ago by two outstanding coaches I had been fortunate to play under.

'How do you think you played today? ... How did you arrive at that thinking? ... Can I give you some feedback? ... The good news is we have a week to work on that and I can't wait to see the improvement next game.'

Using the three-step system I coached three basketball premierships, two winning cricket seasons and a football premiership in a perfect, undefeated season. I don't list these achievements to boast but rather to impress on you the power of quality communication. The football side that enjoyed the perfect season had won very few games in their previous seasons. By simply asking each player what they thought a successful season *looked like* to them personally, then coaching them to that belief, we were able to achieve ultimate success. That was not just about winning the premiership cup, but about each player getting out of the season exactly what they wanted. Less than a third of the team wanted to win the premiership. The majority wanted to achieve much simpler outcomes, such as kicking a goal, taking a big mark or making Mum and Dad proud.

I have the greatest respect for parents who take on a coaching role of a team that their child plays in. It can be challenging to coach your own child — tough if they are one of the better performers; even tougher, I suspect, if they are one of the less talented players. Combine that with the expectations of other parents who believe their child deserves more game time or should be played in a different position, and the pressure can quickly mount on a coach, who probably started out with good intentions and now feels like a politician who has lost control of the Senate.

When it comes to communicating to your child as a coach, you have to be very careful. If you get this right, the rewards are outstanding and strengthen your relationship. If you get it wrong, you can do serious damage to your relationship with them, not only as a coach but more importantly as a parent.

You can often fall into the trap of praising their performance no matter how they played the game. This is a natural thing to do as we all love our children and want to be supportive parents. The problem is that if your child knows in their own heart they did not perform well, they will form the belief that you are giving them false praise. From that day on they will take everything you say with a grain of salt, which is challenging for a coach and dangerous for a parent.

Even worse, when you question their performance you run the risk of driving a wedge between the two of you. Be very careful when you start a conversation with your child as their coach with the words, 'What were you thinking when …?' You might have valid reasons and the best intentions for asking the question. It is, however, more than probable that they will hear it differently and form the belief that, 'No matter what I do, it's not good enough for Dad [or Mum, as the case may be].' Especially if they believe they gave their best.

In either case, if your child forms the belief that you are just being a parent who praises them no matter what their performance level or, worse, that no matter what they do they can never please you, then you have a communication problem. Even more, you have a parenting problem!

Remember, it is important to tune in before you broadcast. 'How do you think you went today?'

My approach was to find out what every player, including my own child, wanted from the season ahead. If I could deliver the opportunity for that player to take the mark, kick the goal, make the basket, hit a six, or make Mum and Dad proud, while maintaining their self-esteem, my coaching would have been successful no matter where we finished on the ladder. I always wanted to know my own child's main goal for the season ahead so I could coach him towards its attainment.

SUCCESS IS DISCOVERING YOUR TEAM'S PERSONAL GOALS AND PROVIDING OPPORTUNITIES TO ACHIEVE THEM.

I used the same approach in our real estate business. During my weekly one-on-one with each team member I would always begin with, 'How do you think you've gone this past week?' If their response suggested to me they were in fantasyland, I would help them tune in to the reality channel. I would then communicate to them my belief about their current results and inspire them to achieve their next level over the course of the coming week, month, quarter, half year and 12-month period.

Whether you are a business leader, a school teacher, a coach or a parent, it is incumbent on you to help the people you lead to tune in to the reality channel. Arguably the greatest leadership role you'll ever play is as a parent. I believe it's every parent's obligation to lead their children towards becoming the very best version of themselves. Not necessarily the version they see when they look in the mirror or read on their social media feeds. The mirror does not always reflect reality, either positive or negative. They need to understand that things are never as bad as they seem, but at the same time to recognise when they are getting ahead of themselves. If you can influence their thinking towards the middle line of realism, getting the balance right through skilful communication, you can't go wrong.

A reality channel checklist

- [ ] Simplify your communication using the three-step process. 'How do you think you went today? ... How did you arrive at that thinking? ... Can I give you some feedback?'

- [ ] Communicate how it is ('This is what I saw') and inspire them to do better. Reinforcing self-esteem is the goal.

- ☐ As a parent or leader, understand the importance of tuning in before you broadcast.

- ☐ Help them tune in to the reality channel by having them share their hopes, dreams and goals, then coach them to achieve these goals and become the best version of themselves they can be.

- ☐ Successful communication is identifying what the other person is seeking from the relationship and helping them to achieve it.

- ☐ Teachers know they've made a significant difference only when they receive direct feedback. Is there a former/current teacher you need to connect with to show your appreciation?

This chapter at a glance

You can best inspire your key people, family and friends by encouraging them to adjust their personal programming and to tune in to the reality channel. Give praise where it is warranted and encourage greater effort where it is needed, but never do so at the expense of their self-esteem. This is particularly important when dealing with children. Help them to understand the reality of their present situation while communicating a firm belief that they can achieve their future hopes and dreams.

100 per cent of your success comes from your ability to communicate.

_____

CHAPTER 4
Become an active listener

To be a great communicator you must develop great listening skills. This was a lesson that did not come easily to me, as I can often talk a glass eye to sleep.

People regularly seek me out to speak at conferences, seminars or retreats. You might think I would respond to any such enquiry with a simple yes. After all, I'm a public speaker — it's what I'm paid to do. Yet after 1500-plus successful engagements over more than two decades, I can honestly say I have never once broadcast that simple reply to an initial invitation.

I understand that 100 per cent of my success comes from my ability to connect instantly with the prospect. So I immediately ask three key questions: Why? What? and How? The answers to these three leading questions will allow me to make an informed decision on whether this is a conversation I should spend major or minor time on.

THE WORDS LISTEN AND SILENT HAVE THE SAME LETTERS.

Listen for the cues

As explained in chapter 2, it is important to 'tune in' before you broadcast. If you ask the right questions, you'll know how to respond in a considered way based on the answers you receive. This helps you to engage in a higher quality of communication. It will come as no surprise to you that I follow a three-step process when *actively listening* in every conversation. This process involves the why, what and how questions:

» 'Thank you for connecting. Can I ask *why* you have chosen/are considering me?' How they answer this strategic question determines what I do next. If I get a positive response such as, 'We have been referred to you' or 'We liked the content on your website,' I quickly follow up with ...

» '*What* is most important to you in hiring a speaker?' The answer to this question often reveals their selection criteria. Armed with the answers to my why and what questions I complete the trifecta with ...

» '*How* soon will you be making a decision on your speaker lineup?' The answer to this question gives me their time frame. And more often than not, the way in which they answer it reveals their personality colour (see chapter 2).

Here I follow the example of any good medical practitioner. The doctor will spend the first part of a medical consultation in 'qualifying' the patient: 'What can I help you with today?' Succeeding questions might include: 'How long have you been feeling ill?', 'On a scale of 1 to 10, what is your level of pain?', 'How does this pain manifest?' and 'How long have you had it for?' This 'qualifying process' helps the doctor to decide on what course of action to take.

In a similar way, when setting up my speaking engagements I conduct a thorough diagnosis before I prescribe the course of action moving forward. I have a module of questions I can reference depending on who is making the enquiry and the industry they work in. Their answers to my why, what and how questions will reveal much about the motivation, values and personality traits of the decision maker involved. All I have to do is listen for the cues. My top 10 questions are:

1. Why have you chosen/are you considering me for your event?

2. What specifically do you know about me/us?

3. What are you looking for in a speaker for your event?

4. How long would you like me to speak for?

5. What's the most important message you want communicated at your event?

6. How best do you think I might deliver that message?

7. What do you require from me/us to help you make a better decision?

8. How soon will you be making a final decision on your choice of speaker/s?

9. What is the theme of your conference?

10. Why did you choose that theme?

Obviously I don't ask all of these 10 questions. I will use a combination of two or three of them and listen for a pattern of language (visual, auditory and feeling words) that I can feed back to them in my responses. Once I have an understanding of what it is they are trying to achieve with their event, I ask two final questions:

» What budget are you working within?

» What would have to happen in order for you to give me/us the go-ahead?

The power here is not so much in the questions themselves as in what you can glean from the answers provided. There is real purpose behind my 'quality qualifying module of questions', and by really listening to the answers they elicit, you will gain a deeper understanding of your client's needs. This puts you in the best position to help them achieve their ideal outcome and be a part of a quality information exchange.

Start with why

Simon Sinek, the author of *Start with Why*, has had more than 33 million views of his TED talk in which he reveals the DNA code of the 'Golden Circle'. Put simply, he describes what he believes separates great leaders, leading companies and influential people from average performers. The common thread among the winners is they all start with why. 'This is *why* we do what we do. This is *what* we do. Here's *how* this benefits you.' Compare this strategic approach with how average companies, leaders and individuals attempt to influence others: 'This is what we do. This is how we do it.' They rarely communicate *why* they do it. (You can watch this TED talk in the time it can take to order and drink a coffee, so make the time today.)

Here's another example of the power of why.

I am often asked to coach someone on their public speaking skills. Some people find they need to develop this skill before they can take the next step up the corporate ladder. Others may have been asked to give a speech at a family wedding, a milestone birthday or some other important one-off occasion. More often than not they will ask me directly, 'Can you help me speak in public?' The simple answer is yes, but I don't lead off that way. I always start off with, 'Can I ask why?' They proceed to tell me what they have to do, but I'm more interested in learning why they need to do it.

HOW DOES THE MAGICIAN PULL THE RABBIT OUT OF THE HAT? HE PUTS IT IN THERE IN THE FIRST PLACE.

The late, great Jim Rohn explains it best in his timeless works *The Seasons of Life* and *The Five Major Pieces to the Life Puzzle* when he talks about 'nitty-gritty reasons': 'Reasons come first and answers come second. If you want more answers find more reasons. If you find enough reasons, you'll find enough answers.' Sage advice from the wisest man and mentor I ever knew and had in my life. Again, any time invested in reading, watching or listening to Jim Rohn is a great investment in your own personal development.

The hidden power of why, what and how

Almost all enquiries requesting my help with public speaking are from people who would rather die than speak in public. Indeed, they seem to imply they would rather be in the casket than delivering the eulogy at a funeral! Having shared with them this new understanding (which I'm pretty sure I learned from comic genius Jerry Seinfeld), I get straight to work on finding their main reasons, then use their answers to my why questions as leverage to get them to do *what* is needed!

Parents who have to give a speech at their child's wedding are the easiest to coach around this concept. Clearly parents will pay almost any price when it comes to their children. Once it is established *why* they want to deliver a speech that lets their child know how proud they are and how much they love them, I take these two powerful motivations and get them to focus on *what* they need to do. This allows them to speak from the heart, rather than from fear. It's a classic case of the heart ruling the head. Once they have established the *why* and *what* part of their speech, the *how* takes care of itself. Once they add in some humour and personal stories around this time-tested system, it is my experience that they no longer fear speaking in public and go on to look for other opportunities to use these new skills.

Combine Jim Rohn's and Simon Sinek's wisdom with my own lesser-known discoveries on the power of quality questions, and you have a strong base to work from on your way to becoming an exceptional listener.

IF YOU WANT BETTER RESULTS, ASK BETTER QUESTIONS.

Once discovered, the hidden power behind the words why, what and how will change the quality of your conversations and your ability to influence others in a positive way. Let's take one last look at these key communication questions.

Any answer to your why questions should reveal your client's motivation level. Their answers to your what questions should reveal what they value (time, money, family, security or adventure, for example). If you are actively listening and know what to listen for, answers to your how questions will reveal their personality colour and traits.

Using this knowledge, I was able to forge a pretty successful real estate career over a 26-year period. Real estate is a pretty simple industry that can be complicated by all the emotion experienced by both buyers and sellers who may be making the biggest financial transaction of their lives. I found that most real estate communication was very 'statement based': 'We have …', 'We do …', 'We achieved a record price …', 'We're number one', '*I'm* number one …' I guarantee you'll find at least three companies claiming they are 'number one' in the market in your town. This type of messaging was prevalent in my market too. I found a winning formula was first to qualify and then to quantify the best way to service the prospect.

'Mr and Mrs Prospect, this moving process you are about to start is less about me and our company than about you and what it is you are trying to achieve here. So I can best help you, tell me what it is you want to get out of the move?'

I found that by framing the first meeting with the prospect in this way, I could separate myself from my competitors and establish a consultative approach. I wanted to 'work with them' through the process, not 'direct' them. Once I had conveyed this I found the prospects would relax and openly share their hopes, dreams and expectations. It was the easiest way to build rapport and earn their trust.

'Why have you chosen to sell now?'

'I haven't personally chosen this but my ex-wife's solicitor has, so I guess I'm selling!'

Motivation: very high.

'Why have you chosen to buy now?'

'We're getting married at the end of year and want to return from our honeymoon to our own home, rather than moving back in with Mum and Dad.'

Motivation: again very high.

'What's most important to you in putting your property on the market?'

'That we get it sold in 60 days so we can secure our next home closer to our children's school.'

Value: family.

'What's most important to you in buying your next home?'

'Finding somewhere that matches our current settlement date of 60 days and is within our budget.'

Value: time and money.

'I'm sure both time and money are important, but if we can deliver on only one, which is most important to you?'

'Well, we can't afford to be homeless, so I guess if we had to pay more to get the settlement we need we would ultimately make that decision.'

Ultimate value: time!

'How do you think we can best get your property sold?'

'Our research suggests that the auction process currently has a 93 per cent success rate, so we would like to find out more about how you run your auctions better than other agents!'

Personality colour: blue/red.

'How would you like to see your property advertised?'

'Oh we definitely love our wonderful view. We would expect it to look amazing in the internet promotion, and we'd also like to see it featured as the main photo of the property brochure. Actually we think it would look stunning on the cover of a magazine.'

Personality colour: gold; high visual.

'What is your buying budget?'

'We don't know!'

'What do you think you could afford?'

'Not sure.'

Colour: aqua.

I found that by following this simple process I could connect with different personality types more quickly and easily than my competitors. Once I had discovered the prospects' main personal value, I could simply pitch to that value and would usually win their business. Again, people want to deal with individuals who are just like them, or someone they would like to be!

'Have I done enough to earn your business?'

More often than not the answer to my question was yes.

'You seem to have a better understanding of our needs and what we are trying to achieve with this move than the other agents we have interviewed.'

If you are in professional sales I'm sure you're aware that selling isn't so much about 'telling' the prospect anything as about 'asking' the prospect everything! Their answers to your quality qualifying questions will provide you with all the information you'll need to represent them, sell to them or work with them.

Rose from Reservoir

There are other benefits to following this system apart from economic ones. You can, for example, enhance your personal relationships. During the early 2000s I was on Melbourne radio every Saturday morning answering call-ins on subjects in my key areas of expertise (real estate, parenting, communication, leadership and everyday life). Hard to fit all that onto a business card! In reality, I was a poor man's version of the Kelsey Grammer character Dr Frasier Crane from the TV sitcom *Frasier*.

The caller and conversation I remember most fondly from that time was 'Rose from Reservoir' (which was how she was introduced by the show's host). I'm not even sure if Rose was her real name or if she even knew where Reservoir was! Callers often felt more comfortable using a fake name and suburb, especially if they were calling about a delicate subject.

Rose got straight to the point. She explained how she was struggling to connect with her teenage son. I asked her *why* this was an issue for her. You might think the answer was as simple as wanting to have a better relationship with her son. Quite shockingly, her answer was that she thought her son was 'doing drugs' and she wanted to get to the bottom of it. When I asked her *what* led her to that conclusion, Rose replied that he avoided her, wouldn't talk and locked himself in his room. By her thinking, he was clearly hiding something, which was a clear sign of his guilt. His failure to communicate particularly irked her at school pickup time. Rose would greet her son with a cheery 'How was your day?' This would invariably be met with an inarticulate grunt!

I had a sense that the issue had more to do with Rose's thinking than with lack of communication between mother and son. She was clearly a red-type personality and I suspected her son was not. Rose agreed to try a different approach at the next school pickup. Instead of asking how his day went, I suggested Rose ask a more empowering question: 'What was the best thing you did today?'

I could sense before she hung up that I had underwhelmed Rose with this advice. As I half expected, she was the first caller the following week and wasted no time in letting me know how poorly she had fared.

'Well, I didn't think your advice would work, and I was right.' (Not one of the more open-minded people of our generation, was Rose!) 'I tried your greeting anyway, knowing it wouldn't work ... and it didn't!'

IN LIFE YOU DON'T ALWAYS GET WHAT YOU *WANT* BUT YOU DO GET WHAT YOU *EXPECT*!

She went on, 'When I picked him up from school on Monday I did what you said. I made eye contact, smiled and asked what was the best thing he did today.' Rose reported with ill-concealed glee both to me and to our wider listening audience that the advice I had given her was an 'epic fail'.

'What was his response?' I asked.

She paused for a moment then said: 'He just said ... "I don't know."'

Given that her previous efforts to start a meaningful conversation elicited only grunts, I considered this a win. Not surprisingly, Rose didn't quite see it that way.

Now my competitive juices were flowing. I wanted to explain to Rose that our mind is a bit like a parachute: it only works when it's open. 'Rose, I'm going to ask you to try one more thing. I want you to use exactly the same approach: asking him again about the best thing he did at school today. Be ready for him to respond, "I don't know". When he does, quickly follow up with, "If you did know, what do you think the answer might be?"'

'Okay, but I'm pretty sure that won't work either ...' And this was where the failure to communicate with her son was formed, in my opinion. It was in her *thinking*, not her *communicating*, where Rose was failing to engage with her teenage son.

IF YOU THINK YOU CAN, YOU CAN! IF YOU THINK YOU CAN'T, YOU WON'T.

I suggested Rose change her thinking from pessimistic to optimistic. What if it *did* work? What would that mean for her relationship with her son? How would that help them to build a stronger relationship moving forward? Rose argued that she was typically a 'positive person'. No doubt she was, I replied. She was 'positive' things wouldn't work out once she had formed that opinion in her mind. From that point the self-fulfilling prophecy played out to produce the outcome she was expecting. If she truly desired a deeper relationship with her son, it would have to begin with a deeper understanding of her own thinking. Rose conceded that this *could* have some truth in it and agreed she would watch her attitude on her next school pickup. She promised to call with the result.

The following week it seemed like everyone I knew was tuning in to find out how this fresh approach had worked out. I must admit I was a little edgy given how direct she could be with her feedback (red-type personalities are not renowned for their empathy and tact). While I have never met Rose, I had formed a mental image of her as the tough judge on the *Idol/X Factor*-type talent shows that were popular at the time.

Fortunately for me, and even more so for Rose and her son, they had a breakthrough moment with this new approach. A calmer and clearly more relaxed Rose came on the air to confirm that for the first time in years she had engaged in a quality conversation with her teenage son.

'Oh my god, thank you so much. I finally have my son back!' Rose sounded like an entirely different person. She explained that when she tried this approach combined with an improved mindset and a slower pace, her son responded in a totally different way.

'I asked him what was the best thing that happened to him at school today. He responded with "I don't know", as you suggested he might. I took a deep breath, considered my approach and softly spoke the words, "Well, if you did know, what would the answer be?" To my surprise a smile came over his face as he explained in great detail how he had made amazing progress in his art class. You could see the glow on his face as his energy and personality shifted.'

For the first time Rose learned that her son had a passion for art. This was an important insight for her, as she was paying a premium for his education with the understanding that he would achieve his full potential in the maths/science area. It was her hope that he would become a doctor. But her son loved the arts and hated physics. Indeed, his art classes were the only two periods a week he enjoyed. He just didn't know how to communicate this to her. So he had followed his passion in secret, knowing it would not please his mother, especially given the sacrifices she was making to support his private education.

Rose had begun by suspecting her son of taking drugs; now she knew he had actually been hiding his art supplies so he could secretly work on his portfolio late at night. With this revelation, and after they had talked for a long time, they agreed on a radical change to his subject selections at school. Rose would ensure he had every opportunity to pursue his artistic passion. She discovered for the first time that she had a very talented son, even if he was never going to be a doctor. More importantly, Rose discovered the key to unlocking her relationship with her son.

Unlock quality communication

There are many definitions of success. It can be associated with economic achievements, awards, trophies, certificates, degrees and titles. Some use their group certificates and financial status to validate their success. A person with a million dollars in the bank can claim to be financially successful. A single mother with a magical relationship with her son has wealth beyond measure. It all comes down to what you value most in your life. No-one wants to be the richest person in the graveyard, but financial poverty limits your choices in the game of life. The communication skills I discuss in this book are not limited to economic or business or personal success. Everyone wants to develop quality relationships. By following the advice in this chapter, you will unlock more quality in your life than you thought possible.

Inspired by the experience with Rose all those years ago, we recorded a program called 'The Parenting Puzzle' that articulated in greater detail quality communication patterns between parents and their children. I sent the first copy with a personal note of thanks to Rose, although my business manager at the time thought it was actually Rose who should be sending me the note of thanks, given the outcome. It was a fair point, but it has always been my firm belief that the two most underrated and underused words in the English language are *thank you*! Whether you are the instigator or the beneficiary of quality communication, you should always finish with these words.

My good friend the celebrated international author Paul McGee ('The Sumo Guy') sums it up best in his book *How to Succeed with People*. Paul skilfully digs deep to demonstrate that good communication requires us to listen and understand the other person, not simply to persuade them of our point of view! We need to learn how they feel, not seek reinforcement of our belief. I thoroughly recommend you review Paul's work by acquiring my three favourites among his titles: *SUMO, How to Succeed with People* and *How to Speak so People Really Listen*.

We can learn as much from giving advice as from receiving it. When offering advice to others, we relearn the lessons through sharing and articulating them. While they are hearing it for the first time, we relive it each time, gaining a deeper understanding of the fundamentals that we share. As the giver, we are the real beneficiary of this action. And if you help enough people get what *they* want, you can find everything *you* want. Remember, give and you will receive: that is the fundamental value exchange.

An active listening checklist

☐ A key communication skill is being a great listener. Tune in to the other person and give them the gift of your attention.

☐ Develop your module of why, what and how questions. Remember, 100 per cent of your success comes from your ability to connect with others.

☐ Don't spend major time on minor things. Qualify to disqualify unmotivated or low-leveraged people and opportunities.

☐ Find out what is *most important* to your loved ones so you can ultimately help them to achieve it.

☐ Ask good questions to uncover the motivation, values and expectations of the other person.

☐ Giving starts the receiving process. To get more you have to give more.

This chapter at a glance

The most important communication skill you can work on and improve is your active listening. Real communication is not about waiting for your turn to speak, but rather about seeking greater understanding of the other person's view and interests. Ask the key questions: identify the why, what and how modalities. In a professional context, you're listening for the key challenge the client or prospect needs resolved. What do they really want from the transaction? In a personal context, you're listening to learn, share with and care for the other person to understand and if possible provide what they need. You'll find that you too will gain from it, starting with a personal sense of contribution.

Tune in to the other person and give them the gift of your attention.

_____

CHAPTER 5
Energy in motion

A significant part of your successful communication revolves around the words you use. Adding tonality (light and shade) to the words improves your ability to influence others. Successful communication also depends to a surprising degree on your physiology, or body language.

This idea was studied experimentally by Professor Albert Mehrabian at UCLA in the 1960s. His findings on the communication of feelings and attitudes have been, by his own admission, widely misinterpreted for more than 50 years. Results from his specifically targeted experiments were used to support what became known as 'the 7–38–55 rule', which quantified the relative impact of verbal and non-verbal communication during an exchange between two people as: words (7 per cent), tone of voice (38 per cent) and body language (55 per cent).

If the above numbers were true, we might infer that anyone could understand 93 per cent of a foreign language merely by listening to and observing the speaker. You and I both know that doesn't happen. The 7–38–55 'rule' is in fact not a rule as much as a reference. You don't have to hear or understand every word to 'read' communications taking place in your line of vision. In a crowded restaurant it is as easy to spot young lovers enjoying a romantic dinner as the unhappy couple who appear to be falling out of love.

Professor Mehrabian's study was published in 1967, the year I was born, since which it has been frequently recycled, misrepresented and passed on as a communication fact by business trainers, writers and self-help gurus. Trainers and presentation coaches support the distortion because it appears to dramatically substantiate the point of view that movement and tone, energy and emotion, are always the critical components to communication success. So 'the 7–38–55 rule' was born!

While the validity of the numbers is disputed, Mehrabian's principal conclusions have stood the test of time. The right words delivered with emotive light and shade and great body language in face-to-face, belly-to-belly and heart-to-heart conversations result in a higher level of influence and understanding. When Mehrabian talked about physiology in his original work, he was referencing the fundamental idea of *energy in motion*.

Words as a call to action

The truth is, people don't engage with words as much as they do with the energy you wrap them in. The word 'freedom' on its own has little power. Linked with historical Scottish independence fighter William Wallace (as played by Mel Gibson in the 1995 movie *Braveheart*), and the word's potency is vastly magnified. Roared out on the battlefield to your army of testosterone-driven men while you wave a sword in defiance from the back of an imposing black horse, and the word becomes energy in motion!

The word 'dream', on its own, can invoke the serene image of a child drifting into blissful sleep, white fluffy clouds and counting sheep, or it can awaken a movement with a force that changes the world. That's what happened when more than 250 000 people who filled the Washington Mall in 1963 heard Dr Martin Luther King Jr's celebrated 'I have a dream' address. The flow of emotion from the American capital to all corners of the globe is one of the best examples of the power of words delivered with energy to bring about a cultural shift.

ENERGY IS EVERYTHING!

Indeed, Dr King's speech that day is ranked among the top 10 speeches of all time by *Time* magazine. As is President Kennedy's inauguration speech of 1961, which is one of many great examples of JFK's use of the power of language as a 'call to action'. Another standout during his presidency was his announcement of the moon landing mission. They are just words in a speech written on paper, yet they are delivered with such energy and passion that listeners could not help but be inspired. You cannot mobilise the whole country, and the Western world, for that matter, to pursue a goal as lofty as landing a man on the moon (and returning him to Earth safely) unless you can take people with you on the journey. And the vehicle that inspired them to take the first steps was emotive words.

It is amazing to think that when President Kennedy shared his goal of an American moon landing within a decade in May 1961 during a special joint session of Congress, and again in September 1962 in front of a large crowd at Rice Stadium in Houston, the US space program did not have the technology, the fuel source or a space vehicle capable of re-entering Earth's atmosphere.

FIND ENOUGH REASONS AND YOU'LL FIND ENOUGH ANSWERS.

He banked on the inspiration of what could be as opposed to the reality of what was.

WE CHOOSE TO GO TO THE MOON IN THIS DECADE AND DO THE OTHER THINGS, NOT BECAUSE THEY ARE EASY, BUT BECAUSE THEY ARE HARD ... BECAUSE THAT GOAL WILL SERVE TO ORGANIZE AND MEASURE THE BEST OF OUR ENERGIES AND SKILLS, BECAUSE THAT CHALLENGE IS ONE THAT WE ARE WILLING TO ACCEPT, ONE WE ARE UNWILLING TO POSTPONE, AND ONE WHICH WE INTEND TO WIN.

The power of emotive language

Kennedy was a *visionary* leader. A student of history and an avid reader, he was encouraged by his father to develop a vocabulary of emotive words to help him express and convey his thoughts with greater clarity and energy. 'If you have a limited vocabulary you limit your vision and your future', Joe Kennedy had taught his children. John was particularly fond of a quotation from George Bernard Shaw, later used loosely by his brother Robert during his 1968 presidential campaign, and, on Robert's death, included in the eulogy delivered by his surviving brother, Teddy: 'Some see things as they are and say why ... I dream things that never were and say why not?'

Kennedy's inauguration speech on 20 January 1961, threw out the famous challenge: 'My fellow citizens of the world: ask not what America will do for you, but what together we can do for the freedom of man.' According to respected news anchor Walter Cronkite, it was a speech that endeared him to millions of people across the globe. Cronkite was a unique witness to three key events in JFK's life. He covered Kennedy's inauguration speech. He reported on the climactic fulfilment of Kennedy's moon-landing goal, putting the words to the first pictures that were beamed back to Earth from the surface of the moon. Finally, tragically, he would be there to pass on to the world the shocking news that JFK was 'dead' — that most emotive of all words!

History provides many examples of statesmen who wrapped words in emotion to stunning effect. Two, in ancient Rome, were Julius Caesar and Marcus Tullius Cicero. It is said that when Caesar spoke men marched, and when Cicero spoke men wept. Cicero was a true statesman who dedicated himself to expanding the intellectual and moral frontiers of his fellow citizens. Unusually, he entered Roman politics without an established support base. He rose to political greatness on the power of his oratorical brilliance and his ability to drive change that benefited every Roman (not just the elite ruling class), which added to his popularity. It was his undoubted status with 'the mob' that underwrote his political greatness.

It was said that Cicero could weave words like no other before him. One Roman consul at the time describes Cicero's speeches as *Industria* — *Motus*, Latin for 'energy in motion'. Indeed, Caesar himself once observed, 'Though he speaks to the masses it is as if he speaks to a man.' Caesar marvelled at Cicero's ability to make each individual listener feel as though he was speaking personally and directly to them.

Caesar communicated his greatness through the power of the sword and imperial expansion through military conquest. Cicero communicated his greatness through the power of the word and expansion of the minds of the Roman people. Of these two larger-than-life contemporaries, perhaps Caesar sums up best which approach had the greater impact on Rome. During an address to the Senate, Julius Caesar praised Cicero's achievements in this way: 'It is more important to have greatly extended the frontiers of the Roman spirit than the frontiers of the Roman empire.'

From Socrates and Plato to Lincoln and JFK, through Susan B. Anthony and Mother Teresa, all the way to Maya Angelou and Oprah Winfrey, ordinary individuals have risen to greatness on the back of powerful words delivered with energy. Some have used their political platform to convey their message. Others have used the power of the pen to produce literary works that have stood the test of time. In more recent times, they have used their media and celebrity profile to convey their message. All of them have recognised, as Cicero did, the power of emotive language to create energy in motion.

Focus and energy

Even if your goals are not as lofty as public service, politics, building a business empire or becoming a media magnate, you owe it to your family, friends and work colleagues to learn what these and other iconic communicators have to teach us about how to make our world a better place.

IT'S ABOUT ENGAGING IN AN *ENERGY EXCHANGE* RATHER THAN SIMPLY A COMMUNICATION EXCHANGE.

By understanding this you'll develop a new focus that will drive you to find better ways to communicate old fundamentals within your sphere of influence.

Little things can make a big difference. Take a standard greeting, for example. On meeting someone we ask, 'How are you?' It's only polite, but in truth we seldom really want a forthright response! And only rarely will the other person respond candidly about their health and true feelings. 'I'm fine', they reply automatically. What does that really mean?

Compare that to a greeting from a high-energy person. They may use the same three words, but they will deliver them with much more tonality and body language, which encourages the recipient to respond in kind. 'I'm fine, thanks for asking ... and you look really well!' I get that sort of response most of the time.

Every day I hear standard greetings and substandard responses. A common exchange goes like this: 'How's it going?' 'Gettin' there.' Getting where? Nowhere I want to end up, that's for sure. Or another personal favourite: 'What's up?' (That's a world-class greeting, isn't it?) 'Same sh** different day.' That's a person you'd want to work for, isn't it? *Not!*

I don't suggest you walk away from this type of person; I suggest you run! Life is too short to live on autopilot using the same programmed neutral to negative dialogue that triggers a corresponding physiological response. If you change your body language from neutral to positive, the words you use will match that shift.

A great exercise I use when coaching teenagers is to get them to close their eyes and relax their breathing. Once they are in this neutral state, I tell them to *not* picture three red balloons in a bunch, or to *not* see a red balloon drifting high in the blue sky! Within a few seconds, they all open their eyes and agree with laughter that no matter how hard they tried, they kept on seeing red balloons in their mind's eye! In reality your brain does not differentiate between *do* and *don't*; it simply focuses on your dominant thought. Given this, I teach kids the importance of positive thought programming, with the understanding that where their focus goes, energy flows!

You need to take control of your focus. What you focus on influences and magnifies your thinking. Here are two simple examples.

Think of the last time you bought a car. Before signing the purchase agreement you would have done your research and made a decision on your preferred make, model and perhaps even the colour. From the moment you finalised your choice, did you start seeing that very car on the roads you travelled? I'm sure you would have noticed your preferred vehicle more often than you ever did before you decided to buy. Were those cars there before your buying decision? Of course they were. But I doubt you saw them before the thought of purchasing that make and model was 'top of mind'. It's your brain's way of reinforcing a particular decision you have made.

WHERE YOUR FOCUS GOES ENERGY FLOWS.

Now think of a major experience in your life. If you're married, for instance, or you have ever travelled to a destination you have long wanted to visit, I bet you had often imagined what that experience would look like. Some of us 'see' these images as snapshots or still photography, others as their own home movie in which they themselves have a starring role as bride or groom or intrepid lonely planet explorer. This focus provides us with a sense of the experience before we live it. It's why many of the most successful athletes visualise their performance before the actual competition. Focus and energy are simply disciplines. Focus in — focus out. If your input is positive, your output will reflect this. If your input is negative, you can be sure the output will also be negative. The same is true of your energy. These two parts of your psyche are too important to be left on autopilot.

Energy as discipline

You must decide how you want to give and receive daily greetings. You can stay on autopilot, or you can choose to make a better connection through quality communication. It takes no great effort to live on autopilot. It takes daily discipline to embrace a better quality of life through enhanced communication skills.

YOU HAVE TO START WELL TO PERFORM WELL IN ANYTHING YOU DO IN LIFE.

Since 1997 I have changed my voicemail message *every day*. That's close to 7500 times I have started my day by recording an energetic greeting.

If you start your day with the routine of discipline and energy, you have a winning formula. My voicemail recording will sound something like this:

> **Hi, and thanks for calling Rik on Monday. Sorry I have missed your call but I am very much looking forward to speaking with you on this 28th day of May. Please do leave me your name, telephone number and contact details and I will be back in touch with you just as promptly as I can. Have a magnificent Monday!**

And I'll do it all again the very next day:

> **Hi, and thanks for calling Rik on Tuesday. Sorry I missed your call but I am very much looking forward to speaking with you. If you leave me your name, telephone number and contact details I will endeavour to get back to you just as promptly as I can on this 29th day of May. Have a terrific Tuesday!**

(Or have a wonderful Wednesday ... a thumping Thursday ... a fantastic Friday ... a super Saturday ... a sensational Sunday!)

As you can see, these two greetings are slightly different yet share the same structure. The key is to put a smile in your voice and energy in your patter. Acknowledge the day and date so the person leaving the message knows you have the discipline to change your voicemail daily, and will therefore have the discipline to return their phone call later in the day. Starting my day with this communication routine ignites my mindset and starts the energy flowing. Some people use coffee, gym sessions or motivational music to get the same result.

I'll admit I missed a few days at the start of developing this discipline, and I would have friends gleefully tell me so. They would call me every day to see if they could catch me out, and it gave them great delight when they would call on Tuesday morning to find my Monday message still active, so they could leave me an uplifting message (note the sarcasm) on how they had 'caught' me! On those rare occasions I would think to myself, 'Is that where your life is at, that the first thing you do when you wake up is check on my phone message in the hope of finding fault?'

More than two decades later, changing my voicemail is still part of my daily discipline, like brushing my teeth! The feedback from my clients was exceptional. Indeed, I won business over my competitors from those prospects who were looking for a point of difference when making their real estate decision. Because these clients knew that I had the daily discipline and work ethic to get the job done.

My favourite message was for my day off, which was typically Sunday. The message would go something like this:

Hi, and thanks for calling Rik on Sunday. Sorry I've missed your call but I will be enjoying this day with my family. Please do leave your name, telephone number and short message at the tone and I look forward to coming back to you at the start of the working week on Monday. Have a super weekend.

Even my Sunday message was recorded with energy. People have suggested to me that over my real estate career I would have lost business by telling potential clients I did not work Sundays. I'm sure that was the case, but for me the lost business was a price worth paying to ensure I avoided the dreaded burnout that has ended many a promising real estate career long before its time. And no amount of business would ever compensate me for losing my family if they felt I was more committed to our real estate company than to *their* company.

THE MOST IMPORTANT THING IN LIFE IS TO KNOW THE MOST IMPORTANT THING!

This Sunday message communicated two things to everyone who called me on my day off. Firstly, I was human just like them and needed a day away from work. Secondly, I valued family time and a healthy work–life balance. In fact, this quality actually helped me secure business, as certain clients knew and appreciated that my real estate business wasn't my whole life; it funded my lifestyle and that of my family. While I was in the real estate business, I was also in the business of being human.

It was my experience that most people who listened to my Sunday message would hang up before leaving their own message. I'm also confident that most of them did indeed call back on Monday, and I took comfort from the belief that *not all business is good business.* It's all choice time. First we make our choices, then our choices make us; we make our disciplines and then our disciplines make us! If we can make the right choices and apply disciplined effort, we deserve all the lifestyle benefits that ensue from these decisions.

If your choice is to work seven days a week, all power to you. I was working harder on myself than on the job of real estate, so my job description and economic life changed from selling real estate to teaching successful real estate fundamentals. This then led to my speaking to other industries, professional sports organisations, Olympic athletes, school groups, church groups and charities. The work–life balance I had created allowed me to develop my speaking skills. Professionally, it is this work that gives me the greatest fulfilment.

If you are living your life in accordance with your highest values, then you are successful. If you are bringing energy and discipline to your life, I know you are creating an outstanding lifestyle! If you make energy, discipline and emotive communication your focus, you will enjoy all the benefits of an extraordinary life. That's my wish for you and one of the main purposes of my writing this book.

An energy in motion checklist

☐ Before entering a room, ask yourself, 'How's my energy?' Do you need an energy refill?

☐ Discover what it takes for you to start your day with energy.

☐ Develop the daily discipline required to ensure your verbal and non-verbal communication is as good as it can be.

☐ Change your voicemail message every day. It sets your energy standard.

☐ First we make our choices, then our choices make us. Choose a daily discipline regime and watch your success soar!

☐ Keep looking for how you can bring energy in motion into your daily routine.

This chapter at a glance

As night follows day and spring follows winter, your personal energy follows your focus. The dominant thought you give your attention to requires an energy exchange, whether that thought is positive or negative.

You influence others by employing words loaded with emotion that compel the listener to act — it's not so much a 'call to arms' as a 'call to action'. Your ability to deliver emotional dialogue may just be the most important leadership, parenting and 'self-leadership' skill you can develop.

If you start your day with the routine of discipline and energy, you have a winning formula.

_____

CHAPTER 6
Building the reality bridge

Life has a unique way of educating you when you least expect it. During one of my first visits to the United States in the earliest days of my speaking career, I gained a valuable insight into communication from the most unlikely source. While attending and speaking at a high-calibre conference, the most useful lesson I gained wasn't from inside the conference venue but over a buffet breakfast.

I was seated in a corner booth that was almost as big as the buffet itself. My plan was to have a quick breakfast while I reviewed my notes from the previous day's sessions before heading off to the conference for day two. I remember thinking that although there was some good content in my day one notes, there was nothing *great* there that would make the whole trip worthwhile.

After selecting from a range of fruit and cereal options (which placed me in a small minority, as the horde went straight for the angina section of the buffet), I resumed my place in the 'Royal Booth'. A group of women now occupied the adjoining booth. I couldn't see them, but I couldn't help but overhear their conversation.

One by one, they took their turn to share the challenges they faced in their lives. The topics varied widely, ranging from professional work demands to personal relationship issues and the pressures of raising children — even Y2K got a run. Yet it was the response each contribution received that really intrigued me. At no stage did any of the listeners try to 'solve' the challenges raised. They simply listened. No matter how tough someone's work situation was or how obvious a 'solution' might seem to be, none was forthcoming. By now it had occurred to me that had there been just one man in the group, he would certainly have provided solutions to most, if not all, these women's problems. Heck, I myself had two or three lined up for almost all of them.

The gift of listening

And then it dawned on me. The women in this group had *no intention* of solving these problems. In fact, they all seemed totally comfortable with both sharing and absorbing this smorgasbord of negativity. It was almost as though the mere act of communicating these challenges enabled them to cope with their reality. I found my early frustration at listening to problems that no-one seemed to have any interest in solving slowly gave way to fascination at the process. It seemed to put into perspective an observation I had made many years earlier about my wife and her retail escapes.

Unlike some men, I actually like shopping. If I am on the hunt for a shirt I will always end up with at least one or two new shirts to add to my wardrobe. If I am looking for new shoes, I won't leave the shopping centre until I have found a pair I like. Whether it's a new tie, suit, cufflinks, belt or aftershave, I won't come out of the shopping jungle empty-handed. I hunt and kill my own!

My wife, on the other hand, can spend many hours browsing, trying on and sampling various items, without buying anything, and still feel good about the experience. To me that's four hours wasted; for my wife it's a four-hour break. For most men shopping is a mission. For most women shopping is an escape. Without wanting to suggest an infallible rule, it's clearly a fundamental difference between some men and some women. I was cracking the female communication code by aligning this shopping phenomenon with my observations (eaves-dropping, to be honest) of the conversations from the neighbouring booth.

So my learning began early on day two, well before the first scheduled event in the conference program. Women communicate their challenges to others to help deal with the stress, to be heard without judgement or the offering of pat answers. Similarly, during her shopping escapes, trying on a dress gives Gai an emotional reward comparable to actually purchasing the dress.

At the end of a solid hour of sharing one another's problems and challenges, the conversations in the adjoining booth ended with hugs and kisses all round and many a 'Thanks for listening, I really needed that'. *Really needed that?* You've got to be kidding! You sat around for a full hour cataloguing your problems, all of which remain unsolved, with no go-forward plan in sight. And that's *just what you needed?* Naively, I thought what they really needed was a man to provide a solution! Clearly I needed to reprogram my thinking.

By the end of the conference I faced the harsh reality that as much as the program had promised, my biggest breakthrough came at breakfast that second morning. I had found the materials to build the reality bridge between my wife's daily experiences and her need to have me listen to her problems. I left the United States with a new determination simply to listen in my interactions, without giving way to my normal inclination to provide 'solutions'.

In less than 48 hours I had the perfect opportunity to road-test these new skills. While taking a couple of extra days at home to recover from my trip, I came into the kitchen to find a small gathering of Gai's girlfriends who were preparing to head off on an outing. I soon found myself deep in conversation with one woman, who was contemplating speaking to her son's sports coach and asked for my thoughts on the subject! Evidently he was not enjoying a positive sports experience. Normally I would rush in with advice about how to initiate such a conversation. With my recently acquired knowledge, I decided to do very little 'directing' and instead to 'build a bridge' to her reality. 'Tell me more', I said. 'How does your son express his feelings on this?' And, 'What would the ideal outcome from your conversation with the coach look like to you?' And, 'How do you think you will approach it? ... Sounds great to me. Let me know how you go!'

'Gee, that's great, thanks! It's just what I needed.'

I had simply listened to the challenge and 'put the cook in the kitchen'. Once she had all of the ingredients, she baked her own solution!

HOPE IS NOT A STRATEGY.

When I coach someone, I look to provide a solution based on the information at hand. When my wife shares a problem or a challenge confronting her, I've learned how to give her the gift of listening. That I am prepared to listen without judgement and, more importantly, without offering a solution, is something Gai appreciates. While you and I both know that hope is not a strategy, the gift of listening certainly is.

In fact, it is a vital communication skill, especially when you're listening to *understand* the problem, not to solve it. In my younger days I was egotistical enough to believe I could solve almost any problem. The much wiser version of me grew to realise that not all problems needed solving. Just as each dress did not need to be bought, the simple act of trying them on fulfilled the immediate requirement.

This approach works really well in a loving relationship, but how do you give the gift of listening to a work colleague in the professional arena where a solution may not be on their agenda but is nonetheless a requirement for the organisation? You can fly in the face of that well-known and trusted research finding known as the 'Buffet Booth Communication Phenomenon' (or BBCP), or you can add to the listening part to build a reality bridge to a collaborative solution.

Road-testing the buffet booth strategy

Not long after returning from the United States, and having road-tested the BBCP with one of Gai's friends, I had an opportunity to use this new data in a corporate environment. Leading into a two-day workshop we were running for 80 delegates, we had recruited a new member to our team. During the final 'team huddle' the afternoon before the scheduled event, we were reviewing each individual's role both in the lead-up and during each day of the program. One task was collecting the dry-cleaned suits I would wear over the two days. With genuine enthusiasm, our newest team addition offered to do this on her way home and to bring them to the venue the following day. I was certainly happy to have one less item on my to-do list and thanked her.

My pre-program routine in those days is very similar to my current one. I normally will arrive at the venue at least an hour before the scheduled start. You will usually find me dressed casually in a tracksuit and runners, knowing full well I will probably be involved in the last-minute moving of tables, chairs, banners and the like. At precisely 15 minutes before the doors are scheduled to open I will change into my professional attire.

That day I completed my usual AV checks and noted the arrival of our new recruit. I could tell she was thrilled to be a part of what promised to be an exciting two days. The music was pumping and the attendees were gathering at the entrance to the room, which was my cue to change out of my 'street wear'. It was then that it dawned on our new recruit that she had forgotten to pick up my dry cleaning as she had planned and committed to do. With about 15 minutes to start time, and my suit at the dry cleaners some 30 minutes' drive away, I was in trouble. Obviously we could not delay the start of the program by an hour just for my suit.

You can imagine how mortified our new recruit was. And how thrilled I was. With no alternative, and a nod to the old theatrical tradition that 'the show must go on', we started the program bang on time and I took to the stage in my tracksuit. Looking out across a room filled with 80 professionally dressed businesspeople who had invested a considerable sum of money and two days of their busy lives, you can imagine how I felt. But feelings of frustration and dismay weren't going to get the job done. So despite looking like one of the AV crew, I began with all the authority of someone wearing a hand-tailored Brioni suit.

THINGS WORK OUT BEST FOR THOSE WHO MAKE THE BEST OF HOW THINGS WORK OUT!

If there is one thing I would like to think I can do well, it is think on my feet and adapt quickly to any situation. I began the program with the concept that we are corporate athletes and, like all professional sportspeople, how we *train* is how we play.

I said how much I was looking forward to training 80 people on the fundamentals of how to be better corporate athletes and, as they could see, I was ready to work them hard over the next two days. Amazingly, they bought it. In fact, at the first break I had several delegates provide instant feedback that they loved the corporate athlete analogy, and they thought I looked very sporty in my tracksuit.

While quick thinking saved the day, I clearly had to discuss the problem with our new recruit. There were two aspects to this communication. The first was timing, and the second part was the structure I would use to 'communicate the challenge'. With the timing part, I knew she was already feeling devastated about her mistake. She understood the stress it would have added at the very start of our two-day program. There was no point even discussing the matter then. There needed to be some space between the event and our communication surrounding it.

EXPERIENCE IS WHAT YOU GET WHEN YOU DON'T GET THE RESULT YOU WANTED.

In fact, it wasn't until a week after the event that I dealt with the matter. To her credit she entered the meeting very apologetic, and I accepted her genuine appeal for forgiveness. I did, however, need to explain my disappointment and wanted to ensure that we learned from the experience. 'There are no failures, just learning experiences. I just want us to learn from this!'

The process of building the reality bridge with our new recruit sounded something like this:

Me: When you arrived at the venue without my suits it would have been easy for me to think that you did not care about your role or about me as a teammate. I know we would not have hired you if that had been who you are. But I need your help. Help me to understand what happened from your point of view.

Recruit: First I want to apologise one more time, because it was unforgivable on my part and I have no excuse. I think I was more focused on arriving on time at a venue I've never been to before and dealing with peak-hour traffic than on collecting your dry cleaning as I promised. I spent the night before preparing and planning my driving route and simply forgot about your suits.

Me: Thank you for clearing that up for me. How can we guard against this happening again, because I want to work with you going forward and feel that I can trust you to complete your responsibilities.

Recruit: I think it would be important that you see me write down the tasks you want me to complete on a checklist, then you can know for certain that I will tick off each item on my to-do list. The key will be to make sure you see me write everything you want done on the list!

Me: Okay, that makes good sense. So you are clearly a list type of person. Again, I want to support you, and more importantly I do not want us to be in another sticky situation like last week.

Recruit: I agree 100 per cent.

That teammate stayed with us for a few years before moving overseas into a similar role with a much larger company. You can be sure that she delivered on her promise, and I never had to begin another event in a tracksuit.

The easiest thing I could have done would have been to communicate to the recruit my anger, frustration and stress on the day, which would have driven a wedge between us in our early relationship and displayed poor communication skills on my part. Putting some space between the experience and the subsequent post-mortem gave me a chance to apply quality communication to the relationship. I also discovered that this particular person was a very 'blue' personality. So long as I could see her compiling a checklist I knew she would complete her tasks.

The tougher conversations

This type of bridge building works very well when the person receiving the communication genuinely has the best intentions and simply made a human error. There are of course negative individuals who dislike their work and the colleagues they deal with every day in the company that employs them. How do you build a bridge to someone who constantly looks for ways to blow it up?

ONLY THE TEAMMATE WHO ISN'T ROWING HAS TIME TO ROCK THE BOAT.

You need to identify these types of individuals swiftly and act decisively. Whether by good luck, great staff vetting or superior interviewing processes, I have been fortunate during my corporate life to have avoided these negative people in the main. I can recall having to deal with only a few individuals with this destructive MO. I found each time that the same approach was highly successful in weeding them out of our organisation.

I would haul these individuals straight into my office and start a conversation in which the focus would be deliberately on everything other than their personal performance. I would always start off with the same question: 'How do you think we are going?' They would typically respond in a negative manner, finding fault in everyone and everything other than themselves. 'How do you think we could do better?' They would tend to focus on what the company should be doing, what their colleagues should be doing, and generally point to things that were way beyond our budget or corporate structure. They would never put themselves on this improvement list!

'Based on that, it's fairly apparent we're not meeting your needs as an employee. Clearly someone with your ability needs to find an organisational fit more worthy of your talent. How can we best help you with this move?'

If they did not then move themselves on, I would need to fast-track that process!

It was often the ones who would not share the same feed-back with me that they gladly shared with others around the coffee machine and in the lunch room who needed to be moved on quickly. 'How do you think we're going?' 'Oh, fine.' 'That's not what I've heard from your colleagues.' 'Who said that?' 'It wasn't expressed by an individual; it was consistent feedback from the group.' The next few minutes would be spent on denial and laying blame on others.

'Clearly my version of events does not match up with yours. I think the best way to support you moving forward is to give you more one-on-one time with me. That way nothing can get lost in our communication. So I'll meet with you every morning, 15 minutes before your start time, to review your plans for the day. I'll also allocate 15 minutes at the end of your day to review the results with you. Your production will speak louder than any words, so we'll let your results do the talking. Now once you leave this room I'll be observing your actions, not your words. This will give you every chance to prove your version of the situation is the right one. I look forward to seeing you tonight for our first review.'

If there is one thing disruptive people hate, it's being micromanaged. They may turn up for the first review meeting, but by day two or three they often end up 'sacking themselves'.

I stress again that I encountered this type of individual only a few times. But I had many an interview with underperforming staff in our real estate business that required a similar if more subtle management approach.

Me: How do you think you're going?

Agent: Yeah, really good! I love people and I love houses.

Me: That's because you haven't worked with any yet. The harsh reality of this business is that you're paid for results, not time and effort. So I'm going to meet with you every morning, 15 minutes before the start of your day, to review your plans for the day. I'll also allocate 15 minutes at the end of your day to review the results. These results will be opportunities either to applaud you or to prod you.

For the right people this approach will prompt an immediate spike in their production; for the wrong people it becomes a one-way trip to the office carpark. Moving people on is one of the hardest parts of communication for any leader. Give people the benefit of your feedback and supply them with the opportunity to meet with you regularly to both set and review their day, and their short-term results will determine whether they have a long-term future.

Even with the disruptors who must be 'moved on' quickly, we still need to leave them with their dignity. Building the reality bridge requires the right materials and a genuine work ethic on the part of the builder. Servant leadership demands that 'if it is to be, it's up to me'. I would take very seriously feedback from my team with respect to anyone who might be affecting team harmony with their negative thinking, gossiping and destructive behaviour. But I would always give that person the chance to share their reality. Doing this allowed me to understand both sides of the story and decide on a clear path forward.

Once I had built the reality bridge I would take action to shift the thinking and behaviour of the individual. Sometimes the carpark journey had to be taken by individuals who were well liked by me and were popular team members, but for whatever reason were no longer productive or adding value to our company. This was the hardest reality bridge to build.

Doing what is popular would be to keep you on the team because we love you. But I know who you are, and I know how difficult it must be for you to watch others pass you by with their results and to compare them with your lack of results. We're in a competitive industry and you are a competitor at heart. You just need to find a new arena to compete in. I think it's time to free up your future, to seize the opportunity to make a fresh start and recapture your passion in a different role, team and environment. This decision will not be popular with our team, but I know it's the right decision for you.

When given the responsibility to make decisions, a leader must find the right balance between what is popular and what is right. It has been my experience that when confronted with the pressure to do what is popular rather than what is right, we should always do what is right. So long as you clearly communicate the reasons for your decision to yourself, it's really none of your concern what others think about it. We owe the individuals we lead the right to clarity around our decision making. Nothing more and nothing less. So long as your decision was made with the right intent, it is the right reality, irrespective of the feedback.

OTHER PEOPLE'S OPINIONS DO NOT HAVE TO BECOME YOURS.

Just as others have the right to form an opinion on a decision, leaders have the right not to buy into that opinion. So long as you can build a bridge to the other person's reality you can make an informed decision. Whether that decision is popular or unpopular is not as important as the process by which the decision was made. I explain this point in greater detail in our keynote presentation, Leading the Way.

The three steps to bridge building

Like so many of the strategies outlined in this book, building the reality bridge is a three-step process:

1. 'When I heard, observed, was told, found that you … [*stimulus*], I could mistake that behaviour as indicating that you don't care about our relationship. But I know that this is not you! So help me to understand what you think happened.'

No matter how they answer follow up with:

2. 'Thanks for clearing that up. So let's learn from this experience. How can we best avoid this happening in the future?' [*solution*]

3. 'I want to support you moving forward, and knowing your side of the story will allow me to do just that, so thank you.' [*commitment*]

Remember, you are building a bridge to *get on* with the right decision, not telling the other person to *get over it*.

This is a powerful communication tool that business lead-ers, sports coaches, parents and couples can use in their relationships. Like so many of the strategies shared in this book, they are success principles with universal application.

A reality bridge checklist

☐ Give the gift of listening to others in your communications.

☐ Keep asking yourself, am I communicating to understand or communicating to provide a solution?

(*Continued*)

A reality bridge checklist (Cont'd)

☐ Remember that communicating, like shopping, can be a mission for a solution or an escape from a challenge.

☐ Things work out best for those who make the best of how things work out.

☐ Learn the three-step process to building the reality bridge: *stimulus, solution, commitment.*

☐ You are building a bridge to *get on* with the right decision, not to tell the other person to *get over it.*

This chapter at a glance

The main challenge in communicating with others is that everyone has a different picture of reality. Each individual's reality is based on their own perceptions, perspectives and information. People are bound to have differing opinions. Often these differences cause emotional distress and disputes that undermine communication. By building the reality bridge you can discover the power to change the circumstances at the heart of the matter and reopen constructive dialogue. Just follow the three steps to building the reality bridge!

So long as you can **build** a bridge to the other person's reality you can make an **informed** decision.

_____

CHAPTER 7
Connect through courtesy and gratitude

'You connect so easily with people ... what's your secret?' I've lost count of how many times I have been asked that question. The simple truth is, like anything that looks natural, it's the result of intense focus, commitment and long practice. I have been speaking in public since the early 1980s, beginning in high school, as related in chapter 3, and through most of my professional life both as a presenter and a coach. So the simple answer is that anyone can speak in public, if they are prepared to engage with the process!

People who know me well will say that communication comes naturally to me. But I know I wasn't born that way. If truth be told, I didn't form actual words until well after my second birthday. My parents were genuinely concerned that I had a clinical speech challenge. I basically grunted and made inaudible sounds much like Bamm-Bamm in *The Flintstones*. If I wanted something, I would simply grunt and point, and my older brother or one of my two older sisters would fetch it for me. Given its success, this became my regular communication pattern.

The trappings of royalty

It wasn't until my parents observed the behaviour that this pattern was broken. And lucky for me this 'toddler intervention' occurred, as I haven't found too many successful caveman communicators operating on the speaking circuit. Little could I have guessed that day, sometime in 1969, when from the 'throne' of my high-chair I pointed at a Vegemite sandwich and grunted imperiously at my older siblings, that this was to be the last day of my rule!

I can almost hear the intervention script: 'Riki, we love you but this behaviour has to stop now.' And the shock I must have felt on discovering the harsh reality that my 'personal staff' had been released from my service.

My parents instructed my older siblings on how better to respond to my grunts and finger pointing. (*First we make our habits then our habits make us.*) They were directed to name the item I was commanding and have me 'recite' the word back to them. It was kind of like an early version of a drive-thru experience, where the customer's order is recited back to them by the person on the other end of the speaker. My parents gave strict instructions that if I did not recite the word, they were under no circumstances to deliver the item. My older brother, who outstripped me by some six years and about two feet in height, tells me I had a shocking temper at that time. Doesn't every young royal prince? Allegedly, for some considerable time I would point harder, grunt louder and even scream my commands in defiance of the new order, until the uproar would move one of my sisters to relent! Not surprisingly, my own nostalgic reflection suggests a different picture.

WHAT GETS REWARDED GETS DONE.

By all reports I clung to the trappings of royalty for a few more stubborn days before finally relenting. From then on, instead of responding like my personal servants, my older siblings became my personal teachers. And things seemed to progress well, until after a few short weeks Mum and Dad added the last piece to the 'toddler communication' puzzle. Now I had to add the words 'please' and 'thank you' to my growing vocabulary. As with any new discipline I had to be coached.

Me (pointing at a cup of water): Wada...

Sibling: What do you say?

Me: Pwease...

(In my nostalgic mind I always sound so cute.)

Upon delivery of my 'order' by one of my 'ex-servants', but before full handover:

Sibling: What do you say?

Me: Kank koo!

Sibling: Good boy!

Me: [Beautiful cheesy grin.]

Didn't I just define cute?

Setting the fundamentals

From my earliest childhood memories, these fundamentals of good manners were drilled into us by Mum and Dad. We always had to say please and thank you. *Always!* And this discipline was passed down through the chain of command. From our parents through to my older siblings to me, and by me to my youngest sister when she completed our family. We would keep each other accountable for our manners. I am very grateful for that, knowing that my life changed immeasurably because of it, as things worked out.

When we arrived at a social gathering, the family car would still be running as Mum or Dad reminded us to be on our best behaviour. Only after each of us had acknowledged our social obligation (much like the von Trapp children in *The Sound of Music*) was the engine turned off and permission given for us to climb out of the car. Once we were all inside, Mum and Dad monitored our first exchanges with our hosts, ready to remind us of our manners at the least excuse.

In fact, they rarely gave us a chance to employ them, despite our best intentions. Asked by our hosts if we would like a drink, we would reply, 'Yes p ... ', but before we could complete the thought our parents would interject with 'WHAT DO YOU SAY?' 'I would have said "please" if you had given me another microsecond', I would think to myself.

Despite such minor frustrations, this early discipline around manners has served me incredibly well. It's a fundamental part of my communication process to which I give no conscious thought, as it is in my DNA. And I am not just talking about good manners with family members and businesspeople. I think everyone who you connect with deserves the same respect. Especially service providers.

SOMEONE WHO IS POLITE TO YOU BUT RUDE TO THE WAITER IS NOT A NICE PERSON.

If I'm being 'courted' by someone who wants me to engage with their product or service, I tend to meet them in my local café or restaurant for a quick coffee or lunch. I do this for two reasons. Firstly, I find people relax and communicate more easily over coffee and cake or lunch than they do in the boardroom. The second reason, and actually the main one, is I want to see how they interact with others. Someone who is nice to you because they want to sell you something but rude to the waiter *is not a nice person.*

People who take less than a second to say 'thank you' to their waitress are typically nice people! That's all it takes to show good manners. One second. Those who take a few seconds more to engage with a venue's staff and learn the name of the person serving them, who say, 'Please may I order ...' and 'Thank you' when it arrives are the ones I tend to do business with.

I could rattle off so many examples of how simple courtesy has enhanced my life, but here I have narrowed it down to three powerful experiences.

The first dates back to 1997, when I attended a real estate conference in Sydney. I went in the hope of finding one or two new ideas to take my career to the next level. To say I underestimated the value of this conference would be an understatement.

Learning from the best: a masterclass

The very first speaker turned out to be an amazing role model. He set out to explain not only how to improve your income but, more importantly, how to improve your life by serving 'one client at a time'. I sat spellbound for the whole 90 minutes, thinking how much I could improve with more exposure to this inspirational teacher. He was addressing a large conference audience, but to me it felt like he was Cicero and was talking just to me.

At the end of his talk he rightly received generous applause before the audience flooded out of the auditorium for a 'teine break' (caffeine and nicotine). All bar me! I just knew I had to thank this amazing man personally. After waiting until he had collected his materials and left the stage, I approached him and introduced myself. 'Please don't let me interrupt you, but I just want to say thank you.' Those two words I had first learned soon after evolving from my Bamm-Bamm period.

Bob clearly appreciated my taking the time to express my thanks. How could I not? I told him how much I had learned in the past 90 minutes and was inspired to wonder aloud what type of impact he could make on my career if I could spend more time with him. 'One-on-one' time! Bob's response was incredibly generous.

'Any time you're in my town you're more than welcome to visit me and I'll show you what I do that makes the biggest difference in my career.'

'Where is your town?'

'Dana Point.'

OUR DECISIONS IN THE NOW SHAPE OUR FUTURE.

Later I learned that Dana Point is on the beautiful Southern California coast, halfway between Los Angeles and San Diego, overlooking the Pacific Ocean. Two weeks after this introduction in Sydney, he was personally introducing me to his market location after I showed up in his idyllic hometown to spend some time with the man I considered the best real estate agent in the world. Seizing the opportunity, I had taken 'massive action' as Tony Robbins had coached me to do, not by 'finding time' but by *making the time* to clear my busy schedule, jump on a plane and head straight to Bob's market. That decision shaped the rest of my real estate career and a large part of my life!

After a few short days of spending time in his office and attending buyer inspections and listing meetings, I saw how I could reach a higher level of professionalism by adopting some of his extraordinary qualities. Not least of which was his daily discipline of thanking all his staff *every time* they did something for him, as well as acknowledging their day's efforts when they were leaving at the end of their work day. And if he missed them in person, he would call them and either tell them directly or leave a personal message of thanks. *Every day!* What boss does that?

On day three he asked me what my hotel was like. I replied that I wasn't in town for the hotel but for the learning opportunity that he was so generously providing. Still, he said, he knew of a better place for me to stay, and he suggested I pack my suitcase so he could take me there. His 'better place' was the guest room in his own home, where I stayed for the balance of our time together. What an opportunity he was giving me! I was exchanging a few short days to learn the very best strategies he had developed over several decades of elite sales success. I was a guest in his office, and more importantly I was a guest in his home.

At the end of our time together, I again expressed my sincere thanks for his kindness and hospitality but, more importantly, for our friendship. But I was curious to know how many people he had extended the same opportunity. Very few, he said. When I asked him why I was one of the lucky ones, he said with a smile, 'Because you were the only one from that talk last month in Australia who made the time to tell me that my talk made a difference. And I saw in your eyes that you were genuine: I felt the sincerity of your thank you. The two most underused words in our profession, Rik, I believe.'

Among the hundreds of people who attended the conference, I'm sure others must have expressed their thanks, but perhaps they were delivered (or at least received) more as a polite, 'programmed' response than as coming from the heart. While I had shown courtesy in waiting for him to remove his lapel microphone, gather his notes and leave the stage before approaching him, others had 'passed over' their thanks during the stampede for coffee as they were reconnecting to their phones on the way out of the room. Yet I was only acting as I had been brought up to do when in the company of someone who was sharing something with me.

Those 10 days in 1997 changed my professional career in ways I had never anticipated. It was during this masterclass that I learned the benefit of changing my voicemail message every day, as described in chapter 5. Another tip he gave me was to send five thank you cards a day.

I was pretty good at sending thank you notes to family and friends. But he was asking me to think about the value of saying thank you to clients, customers, service providers and everyone else I had engaged with during the day. The thinking behind this idea was simple: by committing to this discipline you will connect in a positive way with 25 people each week; that's 100 thank you cards or notes per month, or 1200 a year. If you did no more than commit to this process, your business would surely improve.

Today I send thank you notes to everyone I've formed a meaningful connection with in any given day. If I speak at a great venue, I send a thank you note to the venue manager. If I receive good service at a restaurant I send a thank you note to the service provider and one to his or her manager to ensure they are recognised for delivering great service. I've sent thank you notes to Qantas for good flights (that's pretty much every time I fly, because any flight you get to walk away from is surely a great flight). I send thank you notes to hotels, chauffeurs, tour guides, café baristas, my doctor, my dentist, our children's sports coaches and teachers, and anyone else I know who has achieved a milestone in their life or perhaps has been recognised in our local paper. I've lost count of how many thank you notes I have sent in the past 20 years but they must number in the tens of thousands, and I have the callous on the middle finger of my writing hand to prove it.

Like the strategy of changing my voice message every day, I adopted Bob's 'five thank you notes a day' rule without question. Actually, I think if he had told me to quack like a duck, I would have gladly changed my name to 'Donald'.

So the return on my investment of a few short moments and two simple words was to gain the professional experience of a lifetime — and, at the same time, a lifetime friend.

This relationship had effects reaching far beyond my own professional development. Many years later our eldest son was looking to gain some international sales experience. Not only did Bob provide that opportunity, but he was a catalyst in making the experience happen. Our son was accessing elite sales skills from the best real estate agent in the world while also learning life lessons from one of the best people Gai and I know.

'Please ... thank you.' It's amazing how powerful those three little words are. Like 'I love you', they will certainly help you to develop deeper connections that positively affect your quality of life.

The power of the handwritten thank you note

The second example of this power dates back to 1996, the year Michael Jackson was completing his HIStory World Tour with two concerts in my hometown. As you can imagine, tickets were hard to get. Fortunately, I had a connection through my brother: he had worked with him in the Victorian Police Force and now he was one of Michael Jackson's Australian tour security guards. So I asked my brother if he could connect me with his friend, 'Sarge'.

My brother didn't rate my chances, knowing that his friend was being inundated with such requests — 'literally hundreds of people', he said. Still, he gave me an address and a phone number. I chose to connect via the post, rather than the 'quick call' it appeared everyone else was making. I took the time to explain who I was and my request. I said that both Gai and I loved 'MJ', and I made it clear that we fully expected to pay for any tickets he could source.

Later that week an envelope arrived containing two tickets to the first sold out concert at the Melbourne Cricket Ground (MCG). While we knew we had secured seats, we had no idea where they were in the vast 100 000-seat stadium. All we knew was that we had to enter a certain gate and report to the lower ground level. On the night of the concert, we arrived in good time, not wanting to miss any of the MJ experience, and presented ourselves as directed. The 'lower ground' was on the field level of the biggest stadium in Australia.

The usher directed us to the next section of seating, some 100 metres from the main stage. I didn't think the view from there would be much good, but I kept the thought to myself, not wanting to put a damper on the event. Besides which, there were two giant screens in our line of sight, so we would still be able to see and hear Michael Jackson live.

The next usher sent us to the next seating section. We were now some 50 metres from the stage and I thought to myself that these seats would be fantastic. You can imagine how excited we were when we were sent to the back of the first section of seating, bang opposite the centre of the stage, no more than 25 metres from where MJ would 'hold court'. Then, when we thought it couldn't get any better, the last usher showed us to our seats *in the very front row!* This was way beyond our wildest dreams. What had promised to be a great night out became a night to remember for the rest of our lives. Front row dancing with MJ through his complete catalogue of hits.

In between songs I was scanning the stage to try to identify our benefactor. I noticed an individual who fitted the description my brother had given me and mouthed the words 'thank you' (that's how close we were to MJ). The next day, I sent him a heartfelt thank you note expressing our gratitude for what was the best concert we had ever been to. I started by saying I was sure he got plenty of thank you notes, and no doubt got even more from those he helped secure tickets to such an outstanding concert, but I wanted him to know how genuinely grateful we were.

I also pointed out that we had not yet paid him for the tickets and that while our tickets had a dollar value printed on them, I wanted to cover any additional costs he had incurred in securing the tickets for us. I included a signed blank cheque with the note and told him simply to fill it out as required.

To my surprise, a few days later the cheque was returned with a note from Sarge saying, 'Please find enclosed your unused cheque. It was great to see you and your wife having such a great time on the night. I agree with you that the concert was outstanding. I will correct you on one point, however. I don't get plenty of thank you notes. In fact, yours is the first I have ever received from anyone with respect to any concert. I was happy to get you great seats and even happier to receive your kind note. It looks like we both gave each other an outstanding gift.'

Wow! How could we have been the only ones to express gratitude to someone who had delivered such an amazing experience?

Fortunately for us, this was one of many concerts, events and extravaganzas for which we were able to secure awesome seats through turning this contact into a lifelong friend.

It was also awesome to learn later of his own rapid rise up the ladder of success using the power of 'thank you'. When Sarge was an active member of the police force, he did part-time security work during his annual leave and days off. It started with casual work in the 1980s, but by the 1990s it had become his full-time vocation. The story of how he won the contract for MJ's Australasian tour fits so beautifully into the learnings of this chapter.

A few years earlier, while touring Australia, Paul and Linda McCartney had fired the original security team hired by the concert promoter. Answering an emergency call from the now desperate promoter, Sarge was offered the chance to put together a security detail to join the tour immediately in Perth. During this mayday call Sarge asked why the McCartneys had taken such drastic action. The promoter explained that the head of security had made a series of mistakes that had ultimately tested the patience of this rock'n'roll royal couple.

Armed with this intel, Sarge found several willing helpers and raced over to Perth. He succeeded in providing a superior security service by finding out what hadn't worked and working out exactly what would. At the end of the Australian tour, the McCartneys invited Sarge to continue with them through the Asian leg of their world tour. At the end of this commitment, Sarge received a personal handwritten note of thanks from the McCartneys in which they wrote how in all their time in the entertainment industry this had been by far the best security experience they had enjoyed. Here was a founding member of the Beatles saying thank you to Sarge!

The next tour of significance was the Michael Jackson HIStory tour. When Sarge was asked to send a proposal to MJ's management company, he simply forwarded a photocopy of the thank you note he had received from the McCartneys. It was common knowledge at the time that Michael Jackson idolised the Beatles and the creative genius that was Paul McCartney. Despite several other proposals from leading security companies that offered more experienced security operatives and better value for money for the promoter, Michael

Jackson 'ordered' his management team to hire Sarge. The thinking was, if Sarge's services were good enough for Paul McCartney, that was good enough for MJ.

The next tour of note was Madonna. Again, Sarge was asked by Madonna's management to provide a detailed proposal and tender for the business. Again, he simply sent a copy of Paul McCartney's note, to which he added MJ's. Madonna clearly thought, 'If it's good enough for Paul McCartney and Michael Jackson, that's good enough for me.' From Madonna to the Rolling Stones, Sarge followed the same process of sending copies of the thank you notes he had received from past clients to the prospective client's management team, as the one unchallengeable point of difference he could offer over his competitors.

From legendary rock acts to icons such as Frank Sinatra, Sammy Davis Jr and Liza Minnelli to heads of state, Saudi princes and business icons, it seemed that few celebrities travelled through Australia without Sarge at their side providing close personal protection. In this way he built a thriving business on the power of two simple words: thank you! No wonder he sent back my unused cheque — we were kindred spirits!

Today Sarge has diversified his business interests and he is one of the wealthiest entrepreneurs we know. He enjoys an amazing marriage and is a devoted father, father-in-law and grandfather. He loves life. He does exactly what he wants when he wants to do it with the people he chooses to share his abundant life with. He has a level of freedom and choice that most could only dream of. From patrolling the streets of Melbourne as a policeman to travelling all over the globe at the right hand of some of the world's most famous celebrities, Sarge is living proof that saying thank you can change your world forever! I'm not sure I have a better story to share with you on the power of those two simple words.

To be the best man I can be

The last of my three inspirational examples was actually created for me by Sarge. Of all the amazing connections I have been lucky to make in my very fortunate life, this one ranks right up there, and, not surprisingly, it began with a discussion with my new friend and ticket source from the entertainment world.

I remember the timing of this story exactly because it coincided with our son Christopher's fifth birthday. I was talking with Sarge on the phone, and he told me he had secured two tickets to a breakfast meeting to hear from 'the greatest con man who ever lived', who happened to be presenting to some of the top business leaders in Melbourne. I explained to Sarge that the date clashed with Christopher's birthday, and in any case I really didn't think I wanted to hear from a con man. But Frank W. Abagnale Jr was no ordinary con man, Sarge explained patiently.

'Listen,' he said, 'I don't want to give too much of his story away, but I really think you'll enjoy his talk — and the opportunity to network with some of the best business minds in the state.' Sarge could tell I still had reservations, especially because of Chris's birthday. 'Don't forget this is a breakfast meeting', he reasoned. I had planned to have a 'birthday breakfast' with our son and then take him to school.

Reluctantly, I agreed to join Sarge at the event. Before leaving home early the following morning I kissed my sleeping son and whispered, 'Happy birthday' and 'Daddy loves you very much.' I headed out the door with all the conviction and excitement one feels when keeping a dental appointment. As I was driving to the venue my mind was consumed with guilt and remorse. Shouldn't I be with my son on his birthday? Have I put this networking opportunity ahead of a celebration I was so keen to be a part of, even if it was another 10 hours before any cake was cut?

I realised very quickly that if I did not change my thinking it would affect both experiences. Maybe Sarge was right. Would Christopher really know the significance of my actions when to a five-year-old boy the most important thing would be to see his daddy singing happy birthday with his party guests later that day? Could I possibly get the best return on my investment of time and effort if I did not arrive at this event with a clear focus? In my thinking that would be a lose/lose, which I am never into. I needed to clear my head space before arriving. If nothing else, the man I was about to listen to had written an intriguing bestseller.

Catch Me If You Can, first published in 1980, was based on the early career of Frank W. Abagnale Jr, from running away as a 16-year-old to his arrest at age 21 after cashing more than $2.5 million in fraudulent cheques. The 45-minute talk I was about to hear would largely cover the events portrayed in the book. Four years later, in 2003, the book would become a movie produced and directed by Steven Spielberg and starring Leonardo DiCaprio. Frank was one of the most daring conmen, forgers, impostors and escape artists in history. He practised law without a licence, masqueraded as a doctor with no medical credentials, taught a semester at a university even though he was a high-school dropout, and impersonated a Pan Am copilot in order to travel around the world at will, while charging his hotel and associated expenses back to America's flagship airline.

Before he turned 21, Frank managed to outwit (and outrage) the police forces of a slew of US states as well as the FBI and the law enforcement agencies of 26 countries. When the law finally caught up with him he was incarcerated in a French prison where he was treated so brutally it almost killed him. The French prison system, he would later say, had no interest in rehabilitation; it sought only to punish him. After he was repatriated to the United States a psychological evaluation by a University of Virginia criminal psychiatrist concluded that Frank had a very low criminal threshold.

No wonder Steven Spielberg bought the film rights to the book. Frank's life provided enough material for half a dozen screenplays. Now I was sitting in the front row looking at a plate of bacon and eggs and hoping I would gain some value out of this time exchange.

Forty minutes into the talk, my mind had drifted towards my son. While Frank's stories were humorous and some of his deceptions bordered on genius, I still thought the man was a crook and that we should not be revering him. The last five minutes changed my whole opinion of him and gave me a new lens through which to view my own life. In 300 seconds Frank explained how he had completed his transformation from living a life of crime to becoming the world's leading authority on counterfeiting, fraud, identity theft and document security.

The FBI agent who had been charged with his capture, Joseph Shea, recognised fairly quickly that Frank could help the FBI in their pursuit of criminals operating in the counterfeiting space. Frank was released into Shea's custody and he has worked for the bureau ever since (long after his sentence required), for which he never received or asked for financial reward. Frank saw this as a way of repaying his debt to society and serving his country in a positive way.

Frank's conversion impressed me, but it was his account of what had propelled him into the world of crime that genuinely resonated with me. It was clear that Frank had been more of an opportunist than a career criminal. He had run away from home after his parents divorced and he was asked by a judge to choose between his mother and his father. Faced with that impossible choice, Frank simply walked away and turned to crime to survive.

The summation of his talk is still the most powerful five minutes I have ever heard delivered from any podium.

I would hate for you to leave here today thinking that the stories that are captured in my book, and that I have shared with you this morning, are my version of a good life. I don't think those actions make a man a man. I did those things out of necessity and would give all of them up in a heartbeat if I could go back in time and make a better decision. But I have no regrets about running away, because these experiences were a result of me not wanting to choose between my mother and father, whom I loved equally. I was in that situation because a man who I had never met was asking me to state publicly which parent I loved most. I couldn't answer him then so I turned and ran away. I'd do it again today. Many of the stories of my time on the run sound glamorous, but I can assure you that I cried myself to sleep every night for five years. I never went to a high-school prom or graduation dinner or pledged to a university fraternity. I missed my mom. I missed my dad!

The people in my life weren't really friends, as I was pretending to be something I wasn't. Today my sons ask their mother, 'Why does Daddy sit in his study late at night with the light off?' It's because sometimes you have to deal with the demons of the past … and one of those demons is the hurt I caused my mother and father.

The world is full of fathers but very few Daddies. I had a Daddy. He loved his children more than life itself. He would tell us all every day, 'Your daddy loves you very much'.

It shocked me that these were the very words I had whispered to my son an hour earlier.

They were the last words you heard every night as he kissed your forehead and tucked you into bed. He was a fit, solid man who would catch the subway daily. One morning he reached for the handrail of the subway entrance, slipped and fell and by the time he reached the bottom he was dead. I didn't know it at the time. I was in a dark hole in a French prison. The last time I saw him was when I was running out of a courtroom. I never really got the chance to say goodbye.

I've done many things in my life, most of which are documented in a book and about to be glorified by Hollywood. But nothing has come close to the joy, the love and fulfilment that I have in striving to be the best man I can be today. And this opportunity is all because my country and a woman gave me a second chance. In so doing she gave me a family and made me whole. When I shared with her my former life of crime she continued to share with me an even higher love.

She also gave me the gift of three boys. I will continue to honour her for that and always keep my promises. If you cannot keep a promise to the mother of your children, then who can you keep a promise to? She challenges me and keeps me focused on the important things — to be a good husband, a great provider and, what I strive to be every day, a good Daddy …

It has been my pleasure to be with you this morning. Thank you!

There were a couple of hundred people in the audience that day, but I felt like Frank was Cicero, whispering into my ear alone. I couldn't wait to shake his hand and to share with him my deep appreciation for his candid explanation of 'what makes a man a man'. He, in turn, thanked me for my feedback. Frank said he was travelling interstate directly from this event and would be leaving for home in the United States by the end of the week.

Through Sarge I learned the address of the interstate hotel Frank was staying at next and I sent him a fuller thank you card, hoping it would reach him before he flew home. A few days later I received a call from Frank confirming that he received my note and that he needed to make one correction. As in my note to Sarge three years earlier, I had started with the words: 'I am sure you get hundreds of thank you notes …'

'I actually do not get many handwritten thank you notes at all, Rik', Frank insisted. That five-minute phone conversation began a lifetime friendship. Shortly afterwards we were able to host Frank's godson in our home and help his own son during a trip down under. Again, the power of a simple thank you helped me to connect with one of the best Daddies and a world leader in his field.

I am very lucky to have Bob, Sarge and Frank in my life. All three have helped me in my professional life. All three have helped our family personally. And all of them connected with us through two simple words: thank you.

A connect through gratitude checklist

☐ Look around you. Who can you say thank you to? How can you say it in a more personal way?

☐ Everyone you connect with deserves respect.

☐ Discover the power of the handwritten note as opposed to an SMS or email.

☐ Change your voicemail message daily, and send five thank you notes a day.

☐ Courtesy opens doors to amazing places.

☐ Learn the benefits of always saying please and thank you!

This chapter at a glance

Each day is made up of 86 400 seconds, yet it takes only one second to say thank you to those you connect with. That's a very small investment for a long-term gain. Good manners and thankfulness bring great rewards. By expressing gratitude today, you open opportunities to achieve all you want tomorrow. Being thankful for what you have while you pursue your professional and personal goals is a character trait shared by those rare individuals who achieve self-actualisation.

Everyone you connect with deserves **respect**.
_____

Conclusion

At the beginning of this book I talked about my selfish rea-sons for wanting to share these stories and strategies around the communication lessons that I believe passionately can lead to a better life. Like Frank, I too was asked to make a choice between my parents at an age when most kids are enjoying their carefree primary school years.

I don't remember the date but I certainly remember the experience. While I knew my parents weren't happy in their marriage, I had no warning of the rupture that was about to tear our family unit apart permanently.

I was 11 years old, enjoying a typical day at school, when I looked up from my desk and saw a familiar face in the doorway of the classroom. It was Uncle Tony. He wasn't really an uncle but a friend of Mum and Dad's. We had been brought up to address all adults as 'Mr' or 'Mrs' if they were strangers or infrequent visitors, 'uncle' or 'aunty' if they were regular guests in our home. Uncle Tony was in the latter group. Walking into the room he handed my teacher a note.

'Riki, do you know this man?' asked the teacher.

'Yes, Miss.'

'Then you need to go with him now.'

Without much thought I packed my school things neatly in my desk and walked out with Uncle Tony.

'Where are we going?' I asked.

'I'm taking you to your mum and dad', he replied.

'Is everything okay?'

'They'll explain everything when you see them.'

I sensed that the conversation made him uncomfortable. We drove in silence for what felt like an hour but in reality was only about 15 minutes.

Finally we pulled up outside a stark old building with a sign that identified it as the town courthouse.

'Have I done something wrong?' My mind was racing.

'Your parents will explain', was all Uncle Tony could muster.

We entered the building. I remember it being very cold. We approached the double doors to Courtroom Number 2, which seemed to open by themselves. My heart started to thump.

I saw my father sitting with a man I didn't know. Opposite them I saw my mother and two sisters and a lady, another stranger. Later I would learn that they were my parents' legal representatives. Also that my older brother and sister, being over the age of 18, were not required to be present. In fact, we three younger children did not have to be there either, but my sisters were happy to get out of school for the day.

On an elevated platform at the front a gruff older man sat behind a solid mahogany desk. He looked like a giant. My entry into the room interrupted his writing. He looked up and motioned me forward.

As I stood below him, I saw the tears in my father's eyes and how upset my mother and two sisters looked. My father had an expression that seemed to say, 'Everything will be all right', but he didn't speak.

My mother greeted me in an unsteady voice. I could see that my sisters had been crying and that Mum herself was trying not to.

'What's going on?' I asked her.

Before she could answer the judge began to speak in a severe, imperious tone.

'All right then, let the record show that we now have the item in dispute. Let us proceed.'

The item in dispute? Did he mean me?

'Young man, your parents are divorcing. The question of custody of you three minors is before this court. Your sisters have expressed their wish to live with your mother, and your father has agreed to this. However, both parents have petitioned the court for your custody. As you are the object of the dispute, the court has requested your presence to learn of your preference, which I will take into consideration before making my decision.'

I was confused — probably in shock — although I did note that I had progressed from 'item' to 'object'.

'I don't understand.'

'Look, it's pretty simple. Which parent do you want to live with?'

'I want to live with both my parents!' I started to cry.

'Haven't you been listening? You must choose or the court will make the decision for you.'

I tried to compose myself, took some deep breaths, tried to think.

After some moments of reflection I gathered my thoughts. 'Well, I guess … if I have to choose … I'd live with Mum.'

'Let the record show that the disputed minor has stated his preference to live with his maternal parent,' he intoned. Then he asked more quietly, 'Not that it's any of the court's business, but may I ask … why did you choose your mother?'

'Well, I guess she will need someone to mow the lawns, take out the bins and do all the things a dad should do, and I guess I can help her look after my sisters.'

'Fair enough. The court will take a 10-minute recess.' *Bang* went his gavel. He rose and left the room.

I was standing at arm's length from my parents but could not reach out to them. The two people who gave me life had given me *the most painful moment of my life.*

'Thank you, Son, for choosing me', my mother said hoarsely as she embraced me. I don't remember hugging her back, and if I did it would have been because I was off balance, which perhaps best describes my mental state at that moment.

I turned towards my father and saw the hurt in his eyes. 'I thought you would have chosen to live with me, Son', he said with disappointment in his voice.

'*I want to live with both of you!* But I didn't get to make that choice. I can't make your decisions for you and I can't let you make my decisions for me. I can't believe you have involved us in this. You have failed as a couple but worse than that you have failed as parents!' Pointing to my sisters I went on, 'We should not be in the middle of this. We should be in the middle of our school day.'

I don't know where I found the words or the courage to speak to my parents that way. But the pain I felt at being ambushed by them drove me to say *exactly* how I felt. My younger sister today remembers the experience back then as me 'telling Mum and Dad off'. I never spoke to either of them in that way or on that subject again, but I needed them to understand what they had done. My final words at the time were, '*No children of mine will ever have to make that call.*'

That was a pretty bold promise from an 11-year-old, but I'd had enough. I turned to Uncle Tony and said, 'I'm ready to go back to school now.'

I remember on the short drive back to school Uncle Tony telling me that everything would be all right. I asked him how he knew that. He reasoned it this way:

'When I picked you up from school, you were a young boy. I am about to drop off a young man. I know you. I know that once you set your mind to something you seem to find a way to achieve it. That's how you play your sport. That's how you do your schoolwork. It's even how you play board games! I heard how you spoke to your parents, and that's the way a young man speaks. You're no longer a boy … that's how I know!'

I *know* I am not the only child to have gone through this experience. I'm sure many kids have been through worse during their family's disintegration. But such an event can be a reference point in our lives. Thereafter we can become a product of our environment and repeat the pattern, or we can become a student of our environment and learn from it. I think Uncle Tony knew I would be a student, not a product! That has been my focus all my adult life — to be a student of life!

The good news is that towards the end of my father's life two amazing things happened. First, he acknowledged his responsibility for the divorce and the subsequent breakup of our family, and he admitted as much to my mother. Secondly, he was able to reconcile with my mother to the point that they would sometimes meet up amicably with their respective new spouses for a quick lunch or a drink. The chances of this ever happening after that combative day in the courtroom years earlier had long seemed almost negligible to me. But the fact that it *did* occur gave me a great sense of the power of forgiveness.

My father would share with me years later that the day I chose to live with Mum was one of the worst of his life. He quickly added that it was also one of the proudest days of his life. He shared Uncle Tony's view that I had become a man that day. But it is not a pathway I would recommend for this rite of passage. Dad apologised to me for 'ruining our family' and told me he had asked my sisters for their forgiveness too.

My memory of this painful experience almost four decades ago was the major catalyst for writing this book.

I hope the newest members of our family whom I have yet to meet, and the next generation I may never meet, will feel a connection to us through the life lessons we have shared here. I believe these learnings will serve them well, just as they may help you and your family to achieve success in the greater game of life. Because I am grateful for your gift of acquiring and reading this book, I'll end with the two most important words in communication and connection: Thank you!